REAL-LIFE
DISCIPLESHIP

REAL-LIFE DISCIPLESHIP

Building Churches That Make Disciples

JIM PUTMAN

A NavPress resource published in alliance
with Tyndale House Publishers

NavPress.com

For information about special discounts for bulk purchases, please contact Tyndale House Publishers at csresponse@tyndale.com, or call 1-855-277-9400.

ISBN 979-8-89802-029-3

Printed in the United States of America

31	30	29	28	27	26	25
7	6	5	4	3	2	1

CONTENTS

ACKNOWLEDGMENTS

To my parents, who taught me what discipleship looks like.

To my wife and children, who have journeyed with me through all my stages of growth spiritually and my lapses back to childhood.

To the Real Life family and team, God has brought us together for our part of the mission to be a spiritual family who enjoys the mission and journey together. What a ride and what a blessing.

INTRODUCTION

I was in a grocery store the other day, and it happened again: an all-too-familiar discussion. Standing next to me in the dairy section was a man with a Bible college and seminary degree and years of ministry experience as a counselor. When I asked him where he was going to church, he answered, "Nowhere really."

When I asked him why not, he said he was tired of the organized church. He was unconnected, searching, disillusioned. Like many I have talked with, this believer loved Jesus and the Word, but he had lost faith in what he called organized religion. He longed for relationships and purpose inside of a local body of believers who valued biblical theology, but he had lost faith that such a church was possible to find. Oh, he had started his ministry journey as so many believers do: idealistic, full of zeal and confidence. God was going to change the world through him and through the church he would help to lead.

Then he accepted a leadership position in a church.

There he found little intentionality and passion, mostly just people failing to get along. He saw hurting, lonely people in the congregation and in the staff—especially the staff. He saw a semi-organized church that had become an internal political nightmare with little life inside its walls. Few came to know Jesus there.

What had made matters worse was that most of the people this counselor saw in his practice were Christians, many of them pastors. Most were a mess, yet on Sunday morning—in public—they acted as if things in their lives were great. But this man knew better. These same people had been in his office the week before. It all seemed wrong. He didn't expect Christians to be perfect, just real. Changed. He no longer wanted any part of a local church. He figured there had to be something else besides what the church had become. His solution was to become organic—just get together with a few believing friends and shy away from anything that looked as if it had been planned or designed "by men," as he said it.

But as I listened to him, I became convinced that he had made a mistake in his calculations. Granted, his assessment of the American evangelical church today was on target in many respects. There is often too little life in many of our churches. Christians do put on masks, hiding and pretending they are okay when they are not. They fight over the color of the carpet or their musical preferences. The ministry life of many churches is dominated by committee meetings and worship services and counseling sessions, but in many cases these produce little lasting fruit. Our churches make few converts. Few Christians have authentic, accountable relationships, and many are not growing in their faith. Few give, few serve in the church, and most live for the same things that nonbelievers do. When asked, most Christians say they don't experience God when they go to church. Godly leaders are getting harder and harder to find. I know of church planting organizations and congregations who have set aside the money to plant five new churches, but they can't find any qualified, capable leaders to plant the churches, so the money sits unused.

Sadly, we are making a mess of what God intended the church to be.

While many churches acknowledge that they are in trouble, they too frequently come up with the wrong solutions. Some are chasing fads. Others are asking how to modernize biblical words, worship services, or even our theology so it will be more to the liking of the potential consumers. I believe that in the end, all these solutions will only end up dooming the church to the steady decline it is already on. Don't get me wrong: I am not against using words that people can understand or having music that appeals to a younger crowd. However, whenever we stray from God's Word, we will not have God's blessing, and without that blessing, the forces of hell *will* prevail against the church (see Matthew 16:18). Jesus said that the gates of hell will not prevail against *His* church; He did not say *any* church. If the church is no longer His church, it has no protection from the Enemy. It cannot crash through the walls that protect the lost from the light. Walking away from the church is not an option either, particularly if we want to be a part of the Lord's plan to rescue the world. The church is God's idea, and we must seek to restore it to its purpose and blessing. Rather than swing the pendulum too far, let's get back to basics.

Although I can see the same problems my counselor friend sees, I believe he has misdiagnosed the cause of the problems. The problem is not organization. Why do I think he is wrong about this? Because as I look at Scripture, I see organization everywhere. For example, Jethro advised his son-in-law Moses to organize the Israelites into subgroups so that Moses would not work himself to death (see Exodus 18). In the New Testament, Paul lists administration as a specific gift given by the Holy Spirit so that there could be order in the church (see 1 Corinthians 12:28). An elder's job was to make sure that the church body functioned in an orderly, God-glorifying way.

Organization itself is not the problem. And because organization is not the problem, moving to an unorganized church model will not be the solution. So where did the church go wrong, and what is the solution if not the trend toward the "organic" church movement?

The solution, I believe, is to create a clear and uncomplicated way to train disciples to make disciples. In this book, I am going to focus on what should happen in the life of every Christian and in every small group within the church so that the organized church is all that God intended it to be: an army of believers who understand they are on mission with Jesus to see the world saved from eternal separation from our heavenly Father. At Real Life Ministries, our overriding goal is to train disciples who know how to disciple others. In our church, everyday

Christians do the work of disciple-making and fill the majority of our staff positions. We are able to reach the lost in our area because everyone in our congregation plays a part in the church's mission. The people are encouraged and equipped to do so by their leaders.

I wrote this book in order to show how Real Life Ministries makes and trains disciples. My goal is not to shove our specific methodology or wording down anyone's throat. However, there are principles that can be gleaned from the Word that work in any context or culture. I say this because God knew what He was doing when He created His team, the church. You might need to take the principles and then reshape the wording or the application to fit your context and culture; in fact, I suggest you do so. Your team is unique, and so is your place of service. You may need to use different ways of explaining these principles, and you certainly need to develop your plans with the team God has given you.

It is my goal to share with you how at Real Life we seek to make our church a place where real relationships, real authenticity, real teaching, and thus real discipleship can happen. Rather than throw organization out the window, we built a reproducible discipleship process into everything we do. Much of the purposes and structure of our church were outlined in my first book, *Church as a Team Sport*. Therefore, in this book, I want to explain the process we use to teach every believer in our congregation how to be a disciple who disciples others. This process gives our people a way to clearly see where they are on their own discipleship journey, and it helps our leadership team clearly see if we are effectively training disciples who can disciple others.

Our church does not have all the answers, and we have made many mistakes along the way. But what we have experienced in the past eleven years is so exciting, so fulfilling, so opposite of what my counselor friend experienced in the churches he attended that we can't help but share the story of what God is doing here in Post Falls, Idaho.

Come along beside us and let me tell you what He is teaching our church about making and training disciples.

To learn more about Real Life Ministries, how it was founded,
and how the people involved live out discipleship,
go to thestoryofreallife.com.

A MESSAGE TO THOSE NOT ON A CHURCH STAFF

If you picked up this book but are not on a church staff, there is still much you can benefit from. Discipleship is every believer's privilege and responsibility. It is my hope that this book will give you a vision for how Jesus intended to win the world one person at a time and for how He wants to use you to bring change in the lives of people you know. It is my prayer that you will decide it is *your* privilege and responsibility to make disciples, even if your church is not focused on making and training disciples. It is also my hope that you not leave your church unless it is teaching heresy as it pertains to essential doctrine. (If that is the case, you should have already left!) Even if the church is dressed in shopworn clothes and seems somewhat disheveled, she remains the bride of Christ. Don't abandon her. Continue to meet in your church's large gatherings and participate in its ministries, but also do become a disciple who in turn makes disciples. It is my great hope that you will decide to lead a small group and that you will begin to intentionally, relationally, and strategically disciple others.

You can find additional tools and resources at
reallifediscipleship.com.

Part 1

SETTING THE STAGE
FOR DISCIPLESHIP

Chapter 1

HOW DO WE CREATE CHURCHES THAT SUCCEED?

Real Life Ministries began eleven years ago when two couples met in one of their homes and began to pray that God would work in and through them to bring a disciple-making church to a sparsely populated area in northern Idaho. The Pacific Northwest is not an easy place to start a new church. Far away from the Bible Belt, we have a large number of people who either have never been inside a church or never want to go back.

This little group loved the Lord and longed for something more than the church experiences of their past. Church as they had known it was missing something. They determined to pray that a mighty work of God would begin with them. Over the next weeks, new families joined them, and the little band grew. They sensed God was at work in their lives and in their fledgling church, but they also had no idea what the future would look like.

Today those of us involved in the early days of Real Life stand in awe of what God has done. Our little band has grown to 8,500 strong. We have watched more than four thousand conversions and baptisms. More than seven thousand people participate in small groups. Not too long ago, most of the leaders of these small groups were either non-believers or unengaged Christians sitting on a church pew. Several of our members now serve as international missionaries, and a few have started six new churches, with thousands already in attendance. The little band that started out so small in the corner of Idaho is now training churches all over the world.

When you read our story, you might think that we were incredibly fortunate to plant a church in a place where there were so many gifted and trained leaders to make it all happen. When visitors come to see what God is doing here and see our team at work, they often say, "If we had the kind of people that you have in Post Falls, God could do great things through us, too." At this point in the conversation, I love to share the story about our ninety-plus staff members—who they used to be and what they used to do. In our church's administrative structure, we have seven key leaders who work under an executive pastor, who in turn works under me, the senior pastor. Only two of the seven worked in any church before they became pastors at Real Life. The rest started as volunteer leaders, later took on lower-level jobs within our church, and are now leading a movement that is stretching across the globe. There was a time that no church would have hired these individuals (or for that matter most anyone else on our staff, including me) for a significant ministry position because of their lack of formal training or because of their past issues. Now there isn't a month that goes by that someone isn't trying to take a staff member away from us.

In *Church as a Team Sport*, I said the difference between a high school coach and a college coach is that a college coach travels all over the country seeking proven athletes but that a high school coach has to identify and develop his own players. He knows he must start with the little kids who feed into the junior high program, as they will eventually be part of the high school program. Most pastors today use the college-recruiting model in order to fill staff positions at their churches: They hire people from seminaries, Bible colleges, or other churches rather than develop a team from within their own ministry. Churches even hire professional recruitment firms when they look for pastors. Every time a church hires from the outside, it reinforces to its people that they cannot become what is needed for their own church to succeed.

I am not against hiring from outside the church. We have done such hiring ourselves. But I am passionately committed to discipleship within the church, and I am just as passionate in my conviction that when done right, discipleship will produce the leaders every church needs to succeed. God has placed leaders *within* every church because He cares for the people the church needs to reach. These leaders often sit in the pews, waiting to be developed, to be released into ministry, but often they never are. Our churches are filled with diamonds in the rough, and when pastors and church leaders begin to take seriously our mandate to disciple our people, these leaders will emerge.

So why don't most American churches tap into the hidden talent buried on their benches? I believe it is because they do not focus on making and training disciples. They spend so much time putting on a show that they do not have the time to know or invest in their people. Perhaps they might think they are making disciples because their show (large group events, weekend services) are really good, but discipleship is so much more than gathering a crowd and wowing them with amazing videos or good music or even good preaching. I am not against a good worship service; it plays a part in the process, but by itself it does not make disciples. Yes, Jesus gathered a crowd and preached inspiring messages, but He went much further. He cared very much about the gospel message that would be delivered but cared just as much about the process of making messengers who could deliver the gospel message accurately.

WHY DISCIPLE?

Jesus made it very clear what His church should do:

> *Jesus came to them and said, "All authority in heaven and on earth has been given to me. Therefore go and make disciples of all nations, baptizing them in the name of the Father and of the Son and of the Holy Spirit, and teaching them to obey everything I have commanded you. And surely I am with you always, to the very end of the age." (Matthew 28:18-20)*

Notice that Jesus says that all authority belongs to Him. He is Lord. As believers and as a church, we recognize His leadership. He is in charge; we are His followers. As Christians, we exist for His glory and for His purposes. In this passage, He has given us a sacred mission: to go and make disciples. Two things come to mind when I think of this command. First, many pastors and Bible college professors have propagated the idea that this mission is given to only those trained in a seminary or Bible college. However, according to this command, it is the job of *every* believer to make disciples. The church is supposed to equip its people (every person) to be an army released on its community. Second, this command calls us to make disciples and not converts, and there is a big difference (more on this later).

The discipleship process Jesus modeled was essential to His plan to reach the world. In John 17:3-4, Jesus said, "This is eternal life: that they know you, the only true God, and Jesus Christ, whom you have sent. I have brought you glory on earth by finishing the work you gave me to do." It is not surprising to me *that* Jesus made this claim that His work was finished; it is *when* He said it that is worth commenting on. In this passage, Jesus claims that His work was done, even though He had not yet gone to the Cross. As believers we know that His primary purpose for coming to earth was to pay for the sins of all who would accept His grace through faith. The Cross is clearly central to His mission. However, this passage reveals something else. Jesus is praying to the Father before the Crucifixion and the Resurrection. He says here that He has finished something. Finished what? I believe He was talking about having finished the training of His twelve disciples. He was ready to release them into the world to make disciples themselves.

Too often Christians focus rightly on the gospel message of the Cross but forget about the discipleship process Jesus revealed and modeled. Again, He came not only to die but also to give us a model for disciple-making that trains Christians so they can accurately represent Him and deliver His message to the world. If Jesus had not trained disciples who could in turn train others, the gospel message would have been lost. No one would have heard about it after the disciples were dead.

You might be thinking, *But we have the Word of God.* While that is true, think about it. How did we get the Gospels? From the apostles, Jesus' disciples. Or maybe you are thinking, *Well, after the apostles wrote the Word, the Holy Spirit takes it from there. The Spirit and the written Word work together to reach the world.* But if that is all it takes to reach the world, why did Jesus tell us to go and make disciples? And why did Paul say to train up reliable people who would teach others? Clearly, mature believers play a part in parenting spiritual children to know Jesus, and mature believers also play a part in training future disciples who will go on to train others.

Discipleship is so much more than just sharing the news about Jesus; it is also about teaching people to obey the commands Jesus gave us. Unfortunately, many churches have not taken this charge seriously, and they are experiencing significant problems. This whole issue of discipleship is critical if we want to save the church from the Sunday-morning show and make it a place where real relationship and real change takes place.

NO PLAN B

Many Christians believe that they are unimportant to the cause of Christ and that the work of the church is the job of the clergy. So when I ask Christians why they have never served in the church, they often say, "Because I didn't think I could." Yet the Bible clearly states that all believers have been given the Holy Spirit (see 1 Corinthians 6:19) and that we are all part of the priesthood of believers (see 1 Peter 2:5). We are all saved by grace through faith for good works, which God planned for us before time began (see Ephesians 2:8).

Matthew 16:18 makes it clear that Jesus intended to create a team: "I tell you, you are Peter, and on this rock I will build my church, and the gates of hell shall not prevail against it" (ESV). The church is God's team.

21

Those on His team work together under His direction to accomplish the goal of taking light to a dark planet. We are saved and placed onto God's team to do the part He gifted us to do in the context of the team (see Romans 12:4-8). Again, we are all given abilities to edify and help the team be all it is supposed to be (see 1 Peter 4:10-11). These abilities are not for our own glory but for God's. Some might feel they have no real abilities to contribute to the team, but that isn't true. Paul says that everyone is important and everyone plays a role (see 1 Corinthians 12:12-31).

Tragically, most believers do not know or do not accept that we are God's Plan A for reaching the world and that there is no Plan B. Too often our idea of being on a mission with God (if we think that is even our job) is inviting our unbelieving friends and family to church so the pastor can convince them to accept Christ. If we believe that these new converts should be taught at all, we certainly don't think we are qualified to teach them. We have no idea that conversion is just the beginning of a spiritual growth process and that what comes next—discipleship—will determine if a person matures spiritually to a stage where that disciple experiences real change that others will notice.

Because of this view of Christianity, most believers are not equipped to do more than attend church. Most have few unbelieving friends because they've moved away from folks who don't know Christ and entered into relationships with other Christians. Those who still have unbelieving friends often don't know enough theology to answer the spiritual questions their non-Christian friends might ask. Why is this the case? Once again, I believe it is because most Christians were not discipled properly. Maybe they heard a sermon about discipleship once or attended a Sunday school class, but making disciples takes much more than listening to a lecture and knowing right theology. Discipleship requires real teaching and real learning. It requires conversation, modeling, encouragement, debriefing, and practice, all of which need to happen in the context of relationship. Without relationship between believers, there is no model to follow, no authenticity, no accountability, no application, and no support for the journey. These things come through personal contact. And because that relational context for learning is lacking, life change is much rarer than it should be among Christians today.

Many believers who do share their faith are spiritually immature, self-absorbed, or unwise in how they relate to the lost. As a group, Christians are known more for what we are against than for our love. As a result of our spiritual immaturity, unbelievers don't want what we have, which is understandable. If we are spiritually immature and act like spiritual brats, why would unbelievers want to hang out with us in the church? They can find enough drama in their own lives without joining our drama-filled buildings on the weekends.

When a church spends most of its time and energy putting on a weekly show, the pastor is too busy to create a system by which people are being discipled. This behavior reveals that the leaders have a player mentality rather than a coaching mindset. Consequently, Christians with gifts that the church needs, such as leadership, end up taking their abilities into the business or sports world because the church is not training and using them. If making biblical disciples is the business of the church, and business is good, every need of the church will be met. When we disciple our people, leaders naturally develop and emerge.

At this point you might be thinking, *I thought he wasn't for the organic church movement.* I say to you that I am not against an organized worship service done well (the show); I am against a worship service only. A worship service (show) can supplement the discipleship process, but it cannot create disciples alone. Discipleship demands intentionality and relationship—by which each person is invested in specifically. This cannot happen in the worship service.

It is my hope that every church will return to the model of discipleship found in the New Testament. The good news is that these problems can be remedied by getting back to a proper understanding and the practice of biblical discipleship.

To learn more about discipleship at Real Life Ministries,
go to thestoryofreallife.com.

Chapter 2

THE INVITATION
IS THE DEFINITION

Brandon Guindon, who at the time was our executive pastor, and I were in a small town doing a seminar with the leaders of the most influential church in that area. We wanted to get a feel for where the leadership was as a team. The senior pastor was an incredibly sincere and relational man. Before we came, he told us that he thought his church was divided on the direction and philosophy behind the small groups they were starting. We agreed that if he were correct, the issue did need to be addressed.

We started the first session by asking the group of about fifty leaders two simple questions. We wanted to break the ice a little—get a good discussion going—and to discover whether the pastor was right in his assessment of the situation. The first question: What is the purpose of the church? Of course they right away were able to agree that making disciples was the answer. So we asked the next logical question: What is a disciple?

These were the elders, pastors, and leaders of the church, so we thought it would take them about ten minutes to agree on an answer to such a basic question and then we could move on. As the discussion started, it was apparent these leaders either didn't know what a disciple was or couldn't agree with anyone else in the room. As the meeting progressed, I sensed a relational tension that extended well past organizational purpose and direction. This was not going to be easy. This church was sitting on a powder keg, and the fuse was already lit and burning fast. Everyone on the team was pulling in a different direction, and they were frustrated with each other because they couldn't get resolution or trac-tion. If this church imploded, the collateral damage would change the way the town saw the church and, more important, the way the town saw the Lord. In a moment's time, I knew that Brandon and I would have to change our strategy. It was time to start defining words—important words—and we would have to start with the word *disciple*.

This problem is not unique to the church I just told you about. At Real Life, we do a monthly training with churches around the world. We often have church teams sit together, and then we ask each person to write his or her definition of a disciple without talking to the other teammates. In all our years of doing this, we have encountered only two churches in which the entire staff defined discipleship using the same terms. Even though many agree that the mission of the church is to make disciples, they don't agree on what a disciple is and they don't use the same language. To understand why this is a problem, think about how this might work in other areas of our lives. For example, let's say a football coach calls a play, but no one on the team has the same idea of what the team is trying to accomplish. What would happen? Chaos, right? If a home-building crew agreed that they were trying to build a house but didn't have the same idea of what the house was to look like, could they effectively do the job? Hardly. The same is true for churches not in agreement about their definition of what a disciple is.

At Real Life, we believe it is important to have a unified view of the goal of our church—what we are trying to accomplish—so we do everything we can to teach our people what the Bible says about discipleship. We don't want the definition to be any more complex than it has to be; at the same time, we don't want to make it any sim-pler than Jesus expects it to be. We want it to be in simple language so the whole church is able to remember it. We point our people to the definition of a *disciple* found in the familiar passage of Matthew 4:19. In this verse, Jesus gives an invitation to His future disciples, who were fishing at the time. He says to them, "Follow me, and I will make you fishers of men" (ESV). We believe that this invitation describes the definition of a disciple and that to follow Jesus will mean a life change at the head, heart, and hands level of our beings. Let's take a closer look at what this means.

"FOLLOW ME": A DISCIPLE KNOWS AND FOLLOWS CHRIST

From Jesus' perspective, a disciple is one who follows Him. Luke 5:1-11 tells us that before Jesus asked the disciples to follow Him, He did something miraculous: He helped them catch two boatloads of fish. Peter and John followed Him, as did the others, because they had come to understand in a rudimentary way who Jesus was. Yes, they would see many more things that would help them grow in their understanding, but they had an inkling that they had come in contact with the one who would change the world.

In those days, it was a big deal to be a disciple of a rabbi, and I am sure these men were honored that a Rabbi would have asked lowly fishermen. John the Baptist had already identified Jesus as the coming Messiah (see Matthew 3:3), so the invitation to be His disciple must have been especially exciting to them. As Jews, the disciples knew about the promised Messiah, who was to save Israel. Living in an occupied land, Jews of the first century interpreted the promises of their Hebrew scriptures primarily to mean that the Messiah would save them from those who had politically conquered them: the Romans. But that was not all the Messiah was to do.

First-century Jews also believed that the Messiah would replace whoever was in political control as the new king. He would set up His earthly kingdom, and the nations of the world would bow before Him. He wouldn't just come to set Israel free from an enemy; the Messiah would lead them to a new, wonderful kingdom. He was to be Savior and King, and these seemingly unqualified guys had just been asked to be in His inner circle.

As Jesus revealed Himself to His disciples by walking on water (see Matthew 14:22-27), calming the sea with a word (see John 6:1-13), and feeding thousands with a boy's small lunch (see Mark 4:30-44), they became sure that He was the one the Jews had been waiting for. Jesus was the fulfillment of the prophecies. He was the Christ, the Promised One, and truly deserved to be their leader.

To be disciples, we too must recognize and accept who Jesus is, and we must place ourselves under His authority. Jesus said, "Come and follow me," which means that we begin to be disciples when we understand that we are positioned *behind* Him. He leads; we follow. In John 12:26, He said it this way: "Whoever serves me must follow me; and where I am, my servant also will be."

To follow Jesus is to obey Him. In John 14:23-24, He said, "Anyone who loves me will obey my teaching. My Father will love them, and we will come to them and make our home with them. Anyone who does not love me will not obey my teaching." Jesus also made it clear that following Him wouldn't always be easy. He said,

> *Whoever wants to be my disciple must deny themselves and take up their cross and follow me. For whoever wants to save their life will lose it, but whoever loses their life for me will find it. What good will it be for someone to gain the whole world, yet forfeit their soul? Or what can anyone give in exchange for their soul? (Matthew 16:24-26)*

As Jesus revealed the truth about who He was, people had to decide whether to follow Him or not. They had a variety of excuses for not accepting Him into His rightful place in their hearts. Some wanted to attend to the affairs of the world; others loved their money and position too much. Some, after following for a time, didn't like or understand what He said, so they chose not to follow Him any longer. Still others believed He was the Messiah, yet they wanted the praise of people instead of the praise of God, so they wouldn't follow Him.

It's the same today. Many people like the idea of being saved from sin. However, they fail to realize that believing in Jesus means acknowledging who He is in His entirety. Yes, He is *Savior*, but He must also be *Lord*. He cannot be one without the other. He is who He is, and we must accept Him as He is and follow Him if we want to be His disciples. Yet many Christians think Jesus' job is to follow them and fulfill all their wishes. But this is not true. Take it or leave it. It is what it is, and He is who He is. So the first part of the definition of a disciple is this: A disciple is one who is following Christ.

So the disciples were first changed at the head level, meaning they knew who Jesus was (at least to some degree) when they made the decision to follow Him. Those who really were His disciples then chose to make Him their authority. Again, to be changed at the head level means to **know** (head) who Christ is and to accept Him as our **head** (authority). When we accept this truth at the head level, it leads to the second part of our definition.

"AND I WILL MAKE YOU": A DISCIPLE IS BEING CHANGED BY CHRIST

In Matthew 4:19, after Jesus issued His invitation to the disciples, He revealed His intentions. He invited these fishermen to come with Him as His followers, but He also told them that He was going to change them. He said, I will make you into something. Perhaps the disciples thought Jesus had chosen them because of their godly traits, but this wasn't true. He was taking them as they were: regular guys whom the other religious leaders of the day would have walked right past.

Yet He made it clear that He intended to shape them. Later He said, "I am the true vine, and my Father is the gardener. He cuts off every branch in me that bears no fruit, while every branch that does bear fruit he prunes so that it will be even more fruitful" (John 15:1-2). To produce fruit, the disciples would need some serious work. What kind of fruit was Jesus looking for? His goal was to draw people to Himself, and He had chosen these men to be His representatives to the world. He was going to teach them and empower them to be like Himself.

Jesus was going to address their beliefs (head), their attitudes (heart or character), and actions (hands) as He shaped them into messengers who would deliver the good news to the world. He knew that if these men reflected to others who He truly was, many people would come to Him. Paul tells us in Romans 8:29, "Those God foreknew he also predestined to be conformed to the image of his Son, that he might be the firstborn among many brothers and sisters."

Jesus gave His disciples His words as a shaping force in their lives, and later He gave them the Holy Spirit as the Great Internal Change Agent. The Holy Spirit produced the likeness of Christ in them. This kind of heart change is a supernatural thing. According to Paul, it involves a renewing of the mind (see Ephesians 4:22-24) and it produces the attributes of Jesus in us, the fruit of the Spirit (see Galatians 5:16-17) in us. Jesus is loving and kind and gentle and so on. As a result of these changes in us, God uses us to help bring change in others—to help make and train disciples.

Here, then, is the second part of our definition of a disciple: A disciple is one who is being changed by Christ.

To be a disciple means that what you know is moving to your heart and causing change in your character. But the change doesn't stop with the head and heart. The final part of the transformation process ends in our hands.

"FISHERS OF MEN": A DISCIPLE IS COMMITTED TO THE MISSION OF CHRIST

In Matthew 4:19, Jesus told the disciples that if they would follow Him, He would make them "fishers of men" (ESV). They had been fishers of fish; now they would go after people. That's the mission, the cause of Christ: *people.* When we spend time with Jesus—when His Holy Spirit resides in us—we cannot help but care about what He cares about. When we spend time with the Creator of reality, we see things differently. We start to care about what really matters. Our stuff means less.

I once heard a story about a man who took a U-Haul of his favorite things to heaven. When he got to the entrance, he saw U-Hauls and piles of stuff sitting outside the gate. It looked like a dump, but the things left were beautiful and expensive. He could not understand why anyone would work so hard to bring their amazing valuables to heaven, only to leave them at the gate. Just then, Saint Peter gave him the go-ahead to come inside and bring his things with him. As the gate opened wide, the man saw heaven for the first time. It was more wonderful than anything he had ever imagined. He realized that all he had treasured on earth was worse than junk in heaven. Why would he want his junk when he was being given all of heaven and what was in it? He sheepishly left his pile of stuff outside the gate beside all the other piles. Like this man, we place a lot of value on things that, according to the Bible, matter little.

Jesus came to earth to rescue that which meant everything to Him: people like you and me. He said,

> *"I am going away, and you will look for me, and you will die in your sin. Where I go, you cannot come." This made the Jews ask, "Will he kill himself? Is that why he says, 'Where I go, you cannot come'?" But he continued, "You are from below; I am from above. You are of this world; I am not of this world. I told you that you would die in your sins; if you do not believe that I am he, you will indeed die in your sins." (John 8:21-24)*

Here is the point: The people we know and love who do not know Jesus are lost for eternity unless they accept Christ as their Lord and Savior. When we believe this reality, it changes the way we think, pray, and spend our time and money. We understand there are only two categories of people: the saved and unsaved. Paul said it like this:

> *He died for all, that those who live should no longer live for themselves but for him who died for them and was raised again.*

So from now on we regard no one from a worldly point of view. Though we once regarded Christ in this way, we do so no longer. Therefore, if anyone is in Christ, the new creation has come: The old has gone, the new is here! All this is from God, who reconciled us to himself through Christ and gave us the ministry of reconciliation: that God was reconciling the world to himself in Christ, not counting people's sins against them. And he has committed to us the message of reconciliation. We are therefore Christ's ambassadors, as though God were making his appeal through us. We implore you on Christ's behalf: Be reconciled to God. (2 Corinthians 5:15-20)

When we know and follow Christ, we look at people differently. We don't judge them; instead we care for them and reach out to them in love. When we are disciples of Jesus, we speak, act, and serve as He did. Like the apostle Paul, Jesus' love compels us (see 2 Corinthians 5:14). We long to see unbelievers reconciled to Him through Jesus, and we partner with Him in this mission. We give Him our hands in service. Our abilities, our gifts, and our skills are all-empowered and on call for the Lord's mission to save the world. So the third aspect of our definition is this: A disciple is committed to the mission of Christ.

Putting it all together, a disciple is one who is:

- **Following Christ (head).** A disciple has surrendered to Jesus as Savior and Lord of his or her life. A disciple is one who says, "I know He is Lord and Savior and I accept Him as my authority."
- **Being changed by Jesus (heart).** Jesus said we would know a tree by its fruit (see Matthew 7:17-20). He did not mean perfect fruit; He meant growing fruit. As we spend time following Jesus, He changes us internally—He changes who we are.
- **Committed to Jesus' mission to save people from their sin (hands).** Jesus saved us for a purpose. Some believe we are given

a "get out of jail free" card and are free to do what we want with our lives—not true. God's mission is now our mission, and we recognize that we are responsible for our own slice of history. Our hands are for His service.

For more discipleship tips and tools,
go to reallifediscipleship.com.

Chapter 3

INTENTIONAL: TAKING THE ACCIDENTAL OUT OF DISCIPLESHIP

It's the job and privilege of every Christian to be a disciple of Jesus, and it's the responsibility of every church to make disciples. I also believe that the Word tells us that it is the job of every pastor to develop a system that will equip and enable all of the people in the church to be in the relational process for discipleship. The simpler, more deliberate, and more intentional that process, the less time wasted.

I am not suggesting that all of our time has to have a specific purpose; hanging out and having fun together is a great part of the Christian life. However, believers must never forget that we are people with a mission. Most of the time when discipleship is intentional, spiritual growth happens quickly. If Christians are to be effective disciple-makers, churches must not only study Christ's message pertaining to salvation and His purpose but also look at *how* He made disciples and then follow His example.

I believe that Jesus was the greatest disciple-maker in history. As I study His approach, I see three keys to His success:

1. Jesus was an *intentional leader* in every sense.
2. He did His disciple-making in a *relational environment*.
3. He followed a *process* that can be learned and repeated.

In other words,

An intentional leader + relational environment + reproducible process = infinite number of disciples

In these next three chapters, we'll examine each of these keys.

SUCCESS REQUIRES INTENTIONALITY

During my years as a high school wrestler, I had a couple of coaches who were good men but weren't the best coaches because they didn't have a plan for what they were doing. They had no clear strategy; whatever they felt like teaching that day is what we got. What we learned one day had little to do with what we learned the next. But during my college years, my wrestling team was coached by a master. John Owen was a multiple-time coach of the year, and he knew exactly what he was doing and when to do it. He started us out with the basics even though we were all multiple-time state champions. Every year he said the same thing: "Begin at the beginning." As we mastered the fundamentals, Coach Owen would add moves that were contingent on the moves we had learned last. He would not move to the next step until the team had mastered the last basic step. (He stayed after practice in order to help those who struggled. He didn't want to hold back the whole team too long because some couldn't keep up.) As the year progressed, we all grew in our understanding of the sport and our ability to wrestle — we also won national titles. When the next year came, it was the same. The same beginning, the same steps, the same national championship.

After I graduated, I knew Coach Owen's system so well that I could reproduce it as a coach of my own team. Great coaches do not leave the process to chance — they are *intentional* — and as a result, they develop winning programs. Coach Owen was a great coach. He understood his role: to develop wrestlers who could wrestle. He also understood that many of his best would become coaches in their own right, and he trained us to be leaders as well as good athletes.

Like Coach Owen, Jesus was intentional. When I look at Him, I see the greatest coach in history. He understood that His role was to develop players who could play, but more importantly coach. Jesus *intentionally* prepared His followers to go and make disciples. When Jesus returned to His heavenly Father, the disciples knew He had shown them what to be and how to accomplish what He wanted them to do. They were amazingly successful in reproducing an effective, fast-growing church.

At this point you may be thinking, *Well, that excludes me. I am not a leader. I'm just a* _____ (you fill in the blank). When you hear the word *leader*, you might think of an elected official, a military general, a CEO, the president, or, in the church world, the pastor. While those positions represent one kind of leader, when I say that disciple-makers need to be intentional leaders, I am thinking of people who lead by example wherever they are and who explain how others can improve and win in the Christian faith as well. I am thinking of people who have influence in the life of someone else. So if you are a friend of an unsaved person or a new believer, or a dad or mom discipling your children, a man or woman leading a small group, or a pastor leading a church, you are called by God to be an *intentional leader* who coaches others through the discipleship process.

In order to do this effectively, we need to do what an intentional coach would do:

- Know the game
- Evaluate the players
- Create a relational environment for individual growth

Let's take a look at what each of these means when it comes to disciple-making.

INTENTIONAL LEADERS KNOW THE GAME

Intentional leaders (coaches) understand the game they are trying to teach their players. For example, a football coach knows the rules of the game. He knows how many players can play at any one time. He knows what is legal and what is not. He knows how to score points. He understands the skills needed for each position on the team and the different styles of playing the game. In the same way, Jesus knew all there was to know about the game of life, and He understood the mission He and the disciples were to accomplish and what they needed to do in order to complete it.

In the same way, in order for a church to be successful at making disciples, the pastor must understand the rules of the game and how to teach the game to others. It is the pastor's job to *intentionally* equip the people for works of service (see Ephesians 4:11-13). But, again, pastors aren't the only ones who need to be intentional about making and training disciples; so must every Christian.

When I speak of intentional disciple-makers understanding the rules of the game, I mean they understand the basics of how this world works: where it came from, what will happen to it and to us in the end, and who we fight against. They know the goal of this life, the Christian's responsibility in it, the purpose of their family and the team (the church), the proper use of the rule book (the Bible), and so on. Intentional disciple-makers must understand these things for themselves, and then they must teach them to future players. They must strive to develop a biblical worldview and then teach others to have the same.

This will not happen without intentionality. Our goal is to help those we disciple have a biblical worldview. (See appendix B for a list of resources that can help Christians develop a biblical understanding of the spiritual realities behind the world we see.)

As intentional leaders, we must also be able look at our players and evaluate their skills and what they need to learn.

INTENTIONAL LEADERS EVALUATE THE PLAYERS

A few years ago, my son was on a football team. Not only did his team lose the first three games, they did not score any points. The closest score was 34 to 0. The father coaching the team was in way over his head, and he knew it. He asked me if I would help him, as many of the parents were dissatisfied with the job he was doing. Some of the kids had started skipping practice, and others were just quitting. I told him I would come to practice and watch and then we would talk. After the first practice I observed, I sat down with him on the bleachers and asked if he had ever played football before. He had not. He had been roped into the position because no other parents had volunteered to coach.

I noticed that the quarterback was the biggest kid on the team but he couldn't throw. I asked the coach how he had decided which position to put each boy in. He said he had simply told the kids to take the position they wanted to play. What happened next was confusing and chaotic. All the players went to either the running back or quarterback slots. The coach's son wanted to be quarterback, and since the coach had to suffer through being the coach, he felt that his kid should get to play the position he wanted. (Yes, the biggest kid was his kid.) I asked the coach what was more important to him: to have his son play where he wanted to or to win a game. The coach's feelings had been hurt by the grumbling parents, and he was feeling the pressure. He told me that he wanted the kids to win a game.

So the next day we moved the kids into positions that fit their abilities rather than their desires. After that one practice, everyone could see a major difference in the team. They won two of the next three games, and the season was saved in the minds of many of the parents.

Not only do coaches understand the positions on the team, but they are capable of identifying the right people with the right abilities for the right positions. Good coaches also have a good idea how long each player has been playing the game just by watching him. They can immediately separate the rookies from the veterans. They know what each position on the team requires and are able to discern the players' abilities and where they each fit best so that the team can win.

Similarly, as intentional disciple-makers, we need to be able to evaluate where our disciples are on their spiritual journeys. In order to do this well, we must be in relationship with them. In order to better understand what this looks like, it helps to consider the role of a parent with a child. Moses writes about this in Deuteronomy 6:7. He wrote, "Talk about [the commandments] when you sit at home and when you walk along the road, when you lie down and when you get up." In other words, when we as parents teach our kids about the Lord, we are to spend *time* with them and be in *proximity* with them. Time and proximity enable us to get to know our kids well and to learn where they are spiritually and what they need to be taught. As parents, our goal is to guide our children to maturity—to help them mature and grow so that they move from one stage of development to the next and eventually become effective adults and parents themselves.

Our role as disciple-makers is similar to that of a parent, as every Christian is in a growth process as well, beginning with spiritual birth at salvation and then continuing on our entire lives. We see terms scripturally that illustrate this truth. Peter tells us to "grow up" in our salvation and to long for the pure milk of the Scriptures that will help us grow (see 1 Peter 2:2). He reprimanded the members of the church of Corinth for not growing spiritually (see 1 Corinthians 3:1-3). The writer of Hebrews reminds readers that they were still infants in Christ but ought to have matured into believers who were teaching others (see 5:12). In 1 John 2:12-14, John writes to children, young men, and fathers. I do not think he was writing to an all-boys' school or to a men's colony. He was speaking to the differing stages of spiritual growth and exhorting these believers to live in the faith.

At Real Life, we want our people to see spiritual growth as a natural part of their Christian journey, so we tie it all together by teaching the five stages of a disciple's spiritual life.

THE FIVE STAGES OF A DISCIPLE'S GROWTH

Stage 1: In the first stage, a person is **spiritually dead**, meaning that he or she has not been born again. This stage is characterized by the word *unbelief.* Paul tells us in Ephesians 2:1 that we were all dead in our trespasses and sins. Without Christ, we are separated from God, who is life, so when we are separated from Him, we will eventually die a physical death. But this is not all. Without Christ, we are dead spiritually as well. Revelation 20:14 speaks of the second death, which will be experienced by all who enter eternity without receiving Christ. When we accept the good news—salvation through Christ—we are saved. At the moment of salvation, we are born again (see John 3:3-5). The Holy Spirit moves in, and we start the process of growth as a spiritual man or woman. Yes, we will still die physically (until Jesus returns), but we will not experience eternal separation from God.

Stage 2: Every new Christian starts out as a **spiritual infant**. As new believers, they are excited and eager to learn. They know something has changed, and they may even experience a spiritual high, which is great. Their unsaved friends often notice the difference, and infants are quick to announce their new faith to all who will listen. However, in many ways they tend to make messes. They are oblivious to what this new world is all about. They are characterized by the word *ignorance.* They might know many things, but they are ignorant of the rules in their new spiritual life.

Stage 3: As they grow, spiritual infants move into the **spiritual child** stage of development. At this point, they understand the basic language of faith. They can be excited about their faith, and in many ways they are innocent and cute. However, they still act childishly and are often rebellious and self-centered in many ways. Spiritual children tend to do what they should only when they are rewarded or threatened with some kind of punishment. They may do the right thing, but it's usually to avoid an outcome they dislike or to get something they want.

Stage 4: As spiritual children grow up, they mature into the **spiritual young adult** stage. At this stage, they have grown tremendously from where they started. They are eager to serve, think independently, and look much like adults; however, they still have much to learn about responsibility and about how to care for the spiritual needs of others. They are zealous for God and can be characterized as being "God-focused" and "other-centered." They are becoming intentional or strategic about sharing their faith and will see people converted, but they are not yet able to reproduce disciples who can make disciples. They serve intentionally but don't make disciples intentionally. They want their independence, and in some cases they should have it, but they need continued coaching/parenting.

Stage 5: In the final stage of spiritual development, we become spiritually mature enough to reproduce disciples — we become **spiritual parents.** I am purposely using the term *parent* here rather than *adult*. As Christians we are called to make disciples — to do our part to reproduce our faith in another. Adults are *able* to reproduce, but that does not mean they are reproducing. I know many Christians who have the ability to be spiritual parents but don't make it a priority. Though they would like to call themselves mature, I would say that they are not. Why? Because they have not prioritized their lives around the mission of Christ, which is to make disciples. Just as the human race continues because we physically reproduce, so Christianity continues on this planet because Christians spiritually reproduce, or make disciples.

Note: I want to emphasize that assessment is not a way of designating one believer as more valuable than another. It's very important that disciple-makers and disciples understand the difference between *value* and *usefulness.* While a mature Christian is more useful to the purpose of the Lord and the church than a spiritual infant or child, he or she is not more valuable.

The following diagram sums up what we've been discussing.

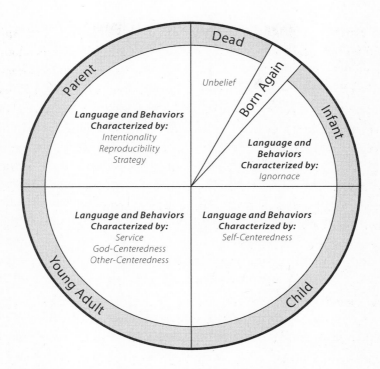

THE IMPORTANCE OF AN ACCURATE ASSESSMENT

Once again, intentional leaders understand the game. They are also then able to evaluate where a person is in his or her development as a player. This is an important skill because, as I illustrated in the kids' football analogy, without proper assessment of the players, a coach can't get the right players in the right places or help them develop further. Accurate assessment is critical. I've found that many Christians have an inaccurate assessment of their own level of spiritual maturity as well as the level of those around them. In other words, many believers are not as mature as they *think* they are. Some think they are spiritually mature because they have been in church for years or because they went to Bible college or seminary. When this is the case, their attempts at leadership often fail. Their spiritual immaturity causes them to be unable to relate well with others. Theology rarely causes church splits; breaks in relationships always play the biggest part in internal battles.

Remember the definition of a disciple from the last chapter? A disciple is one who follows Jesus, is being changed by Jesus, and is committed to the mission of Jesus. As a result, a disciple loves God and loves others. Knowing about and following Christ is only part of what it means to be a disciple. As a result of knowing who Jesus is, we follow Him. As we follow Him, we are being changed by Him. The apostle Paul said that if we know all things but don't love, we are nothing (see 1 Corinthians 13:1-13). Knowledge of the Word and of the Christian life must move from the head to the heart, where it genuinely affects our character, and from the heart to the hands, where it affects our actions. Christians who are spiritually mature are relational—they love God and they love others. Their character tends to reflect the character of Christ more and more. They are servants of Christ and they serve Him by serving others with something tangible. Their resources, abilities, time, and money are at His disposal so that He can complete His mission through them. Again, disciples are committed to the mission of Christ with all that they have—with their actions (their hands).

I've also met other believers who have assessed themselves as less mature than they actually were. They didn't believe they were mature disciples of Christ because of their awareness of their own sin and struggles. They didn't think they were worthy to be used. The Devil loves that kind of thinking. Too often people who have a soft heart toward God forget that even a spiritually mature person (a spiritual parent) can act like a child at times. (Oh, how often I have done that!) Spiritual parents recognize those lapses and sins for what they are. They confess it to the Lord and ask forgiveness from the ones they have hurt. Spiritual children, on the other hand, still need a mom or a dad or a teacher to point out the problem and insist upon change. Spiritual parents earn the right to speak into a child's life because of their growing relationship. Spiritually mature believers place people in their lives to hold them accountable. They seek accountability because they know they can fail. When they have a blind spot and it is pointed out to them, they are thankful no matter how hard it is to hear or change. Spiritual children are often not so willing to be disciplined by others. They want to be affirmed rather than confronted, even when the confronting is done in love.

KNOWING WHERE WE (AND OTHERS) ARE IN THE GROWTH PROCESS

That's why at Real Life we teach people how they can know *where they are* in the discipleship process and *where others are* as well.

Jesus tells us plainly that we can identify a tree by its fruit. He said, "A good man brings good things out of the good stored up in his heart, and an evil man brings evil things out of the evil stored up in his heart. For the mouth speaks what the heart is full of" (Luke 6:45). In other words, we can know where a person is spiritually by paying attention to what that person does and says. When people spend time together in a relational context, when they talk and listen to each other, they are better able to truly know each other. If we watch how a person lives life and get to know that person well, we can figure out what stage that individual is in and what he or she can do in terms of growth and ministry. For that reason, one simple skill we teach our people is to listen for "a phrase from the stage." A person's consistent words will often reveal what stage he or she is in spiritually.

For example, those who are **spiritually dead** say such things as "I don't believe in God" and "There are many ways to get to God." **Spiritual infants** speak from ignorance. They don't know what the Bible says about what happens when we die, or they might mix the Christian faith with Buddhism and say that person is where they are because of bad karma. This does not mean they are not Christians; it means they don't know yet what the Bible teaches about the subject. They need to be taught. A **spiritual child** says such things as "I love my small group—don't add anyone to it" and "I am not being fed at my church, so I am going to go to one that meets my needs better."

When we listen and do this kind of "phrase from the stage" assessment with those God brings into our lives, we get a good idea about what to do next as we train them to be disciple-makers. (We'll talk more in upcoming chapters about what phrases are common in each of the five stages of spiritual development.) The bottom line is this: We can identify where a person is in the spiritual growth process by watching and listening as we live life together, ask questions, and observe each other.

Jesus did this well. Here's just one example. One day He was walking with His disciples and heard them arguing with one another about who would be the greatest in the kingdom of heaven (see Mark 9:33-35). Later, after hearing them argue again about the same issue, He taught them a lesson in servanthood by washing their feet (see Luke 22:24-27; John 13:3-5). How did He know the disciples needed this lesson? He knew because He had spent many days with them. He had listened to their conversations and knew what they were talking about. He knew what was in their hearts, and He addressed what was there. He didn't do so with a four-point sermon; instead He washed their feet. In His willingness to do the lowest of tasks, Jesus gave His disciples an experience they would never forget. He lived out the lesson in front of them. He taught in such a way that no matter a person's learning style, he or she could get the point.

INTENTIONAL LEADERS CREATE AN ENVIRONMENT FOR GROWTH

The third thing an intentional leader does is create an environment where growth can happen. In other words, an intentional leader knows the game, can evaluate the players, and can create an environment that produces change in the life of the disciple. We'll examine this last point in the next chapter.

Chapter 4

RELATIONAL: MAKING A WAY FOR REAL CHANGE

I grew up in farm country, and at an early age I learned how to move pipe from one field to another in order to get water to the crops that needed it. When it comes to discipleship, relationships are the pipe. They are the conduit that delivers the precious ingredients of discipleship.

If we are to understand Jesus' discipleship method, we must spend time talking about relationships. At Real Life we believe that without true relationship, discipleship is not possible. Here's why.

MORE IS "CAUGHT" THAN TAUGHT

Most pastors in the United States long to teach to a huge crowd of excited people on Sunday mornings: people packed into pews, pens and notebooks in hand, waiting for a download of all kinds of top-rate, inspiring information from the Bible. Amazingly, this kind of learning environment is exactly what a good schoolteacher would hate: a big classroom and a one-size-fits-all lecture style of teaching. Classroom teachers know that most people don't learn best by listening to lectures. Yet many pastors believe they are making disciples by preaching sermons that teach their congregations what the Bible says. They see discipleship as simply a transfer of knowledge from teacher to student, and the result will be a changed life. What makes this even less effective than a classroom environment is that church is only one time a week for most Christians. According to some assessments, Christians go to church only 1.6 times a month. No wonder most believers don't have a biblical worldview. Many pastors lament the fact that most Christians are too busy to come to more than a worship service, so they pour all they have into that one venue. As a result, they have created a knowledge-based environment for discipling; they put all the emphasis and focus on the worship service and sermon on Sunday morning.

Don't get me wrong: Good things can happen in a large-group setting that cannot happen in a small one. It's exciting to see masses of people committed to the same thing. It enables us to see that we are part of bigger movement than just our little circle when we get together for worship in a large-group setting. And when we listen to a gifted Bible teacher and speaker, we can come away inspired and encouraged. We can even learn some in this environment. Our hearts are touched as we worship together—the Lord does inhabit the praises of His people.

But remember, discipleship requires more than a head-level change. Jesus said in Matthew 4:19 that He would make us into something altogether different—that we would experience change at the heart and hands level too. I am convinced that little learning takes place in a formal environment alone, which is why at Real Life we focus on small groups that are relational. Most people are not auditory learners and struggle to keep focused for any period of time, especially now in the era of the short attention span. Effective disciple-makers do not exclude formal instruction, but they understand its limitations.

Jesus modeled the importance of relationship in the way He taught His disciples: He followed the Deuteronomy 6:7 exhortation we talked about earlier. God's commands were upon His heart, and He talked about them as He spent time with the disciples. He talked about the truth when they ate and when they went to bed. Jesus was *with* his disciples because His relationship with them was the conduit by which He could deliver all that they needed.

Jesus often used stories as a jumping-off point to create great discussions. He also used everyday experiences such as farming, gardening, fishing, and shepherding to teach deeper spiritual truths. He modeled the behaviors He wanted the disciples to learn: how to pray, how to be a servant, how to be humble, and so on. He pointed out people who were doing life right (such as the widow who quietly gave all she had [see Mark 12:41-44]), and He also pointed out those who were getting it wrong (such as the Pharisees [see Mark 12:38-40]). All of these teaching methods were relational in nature. Jesus knew exactly what He was doing with His disciples. He invested His life in the Twelve. He chose to be in relationship with His disciples because He understood that more is "caught" than taught.

At Real Life we also believe that when discipleship is done in a relational environment, it keeps the journey from becoming overwhelming.

TWO ARE BETTER THAN ONE

My job as a pastor is not enough to keep me going. I love to serve the Lord, and I am incredibly grateful that I get to be a part of what God is doing here. But without the support, encouragement, and help of my friends, I never would have made it this far. Relationships not only help me grow and learn but also give me strength for the journey. They help all of us complete the mission of going and making disciples.

As the author of Ecclesiastes writes, two *are* better than one (see 4:9). Two get more work done. Two are able to stay warm when the world gets cold. Two defend better than one. Jesus sent His disciples out by twos because together they could encourage one another and help keep each other safe spiritually (see Mark 6:7). The early church did the same (see Acts 13:1-3).

But there is yet another reason why we believe that relationship is necessary for effective discipleship.

RELATIONSHIP MAKES THE MESSAGE REAL

Have you ever noticed how often these early Christians spent time together? In the book of Acts, we see that they met together on the first day of the week and daily in their homes. They also met together in the temple courts in large numbers. Like people today, the early Christians were busy. They had character flaws, bad attitudes, and bad breath. They came from different backgrounds and had different preferences. They had kids, work, and chores, yet their hearts were for their brothers and sisters in Christ. At times they were annoyed with each other, but they still were committed to meeting together. They felt that being together was better than being alone in the faith. They had a desire to be with people of the kingdom. Something had happened to them that changed the way they saw life and its priorities. They had something that bound them together, something in common. The members of the early church shared what they had with each other and even with people they didn't know. Conflicts arose, and they dealt with them and moved on.

In today's world of conditional relationships, the early church model seems wonderfully different. The early church was not without problems, but in spite of them, God was working and being glorified and the church was storming the gates of hell. These Christians were committed to each other and to a cause bigger than themselves. Their mutual faith in Jesus gave them purpose and stability—and peace. As a result, the early church found favor with all the people. It was hard to hate a group of people who had that kind of love.

God's church works, but the way the church is structured must support its values. And an important value that needs to be supported and protected in our churches is relationship—relationship with the true God and relationship among believers. The church needs relationship, not just because it is the best way to teach but because our relationships are the evidence that what we preach is true. Let me explain.

God's whole book is about restored relationship with Himself and with others. Jesus made the point that all biblical teaching had pointed to relationship:

"YOU SHALL LOVE THE LORD YOUR GOD WITH ALL YOUR HEART, AND WITH ALL YOUR SOUL, AND WITH ALL YOUR MIND." *This is the great*

and foremost commandment. The second is like it, "YOU SHALL
LOVE YOUR NEIGHBOR AS YOURSELF." On these two commandments
depend the whole Law and the Prophets. (Matthew 22:37-40, NASB)

Jesus also made it clear that people would know that we were His disciples by our love for one another (see John 13:34-35). He didn't say the world would know we are Christians because we are theologically right, though we should be. He didn't say people would know we are Christians because of miracles, though sometimes God uses them. He didn't say people would know we are believers because we are wealthy and disease-free, though God sometimes blesses His people in these ways. Jesus said we would be known by our love.

I remember when I used to mock Christians because they would always talk about Jesus as the Prince of Peace and quote Galatians 5:22-23, saying that one of the evidences for Christianity is the spiritual fruit of love and peace. But I didn't see much evidence of this in the lives of the Christians I knew. If this Jesus thing didn't work for even them, why would I want it in my life? I had seen too many Christians splitting churches, fighting with each other over music, the color of the carpet, and denominational differences. I knew I needed and wanted positive relationships, but I just didn't think I could find them in Christianity.

However, experience has convinced me that I was wrong. When the structure of a church supports a relational environment for discipleship (spiritual growth), that church is more likely to be full of people who demonstrate this kind of love Christ talked about. True relationships with other believers can give us the support and accountability we need to change and grow in our love for God and others. True relationship gives nonbelievers a picture of what Jesus can do in and for them. Jesus really does offer us peace, and it is like water to a thirsty soul. Most people know they need love. Musicians are constantly writing songs about our desire and need for it. It's just that most folks are looking in all the wrong places. When they see they can find in our churches what they know they need, their hearts soften and doors are opened.

Okay, I think I have made the point about the *need* for relationship. Now let's turn our attention to what makes a relational environment. Jesus remains our standard for not only *what* to teach but also *how* to teach. At Real Life we believe that in a good growth environment there is shepherding, transparency, accountability, and guided practice.

WHAT MAKES A RELATIONAL ENVIRONMENT FOR DISCIPLESHIP?

Real Teaching

Remember that every disciple needs to replace the world's perspective (which he or she starts out with) with God's perspective. We need a biblical worldview. The Bible is God's scrub brush, designed to sanctify (cleanse) us (see John 17:17). His Word is also the spiritual food that sustains our spiritual life (see Matthew 4:4). It lights our path (see Psalm 119:105), and we are to hide God's Word in our hearts that we might not sin against Him (see Psalm 119:11). It is also our sword of the Spirit, which we use to fight the Enemy (see Ephesians 6:17).

I often hear people say that our church is about small groups. I disagree. We are about discipleship, and we believe it happens best in small groups. Our small groups are not designed to shut our back door or to get people into relationships. Our small groups are the conduit for real discipleship, which includes real teaching. Real teaching from the Word. The right kind of teaching explains the Word so that those in the group can understand it right where they are, whatever their stage of spiritual growth. There are many illustrations used, with many questions answered. There is modeling so that the right definitions of words can be seen. There is proper application to the lives of those in the group because the leader knows them well.

Shepherding

Just as a new mother needs to take care of her baby, a disciple-maker who helps a spiritually dead person come to faith needs to help that spiritual infant grow up. Spiritual infants don't understand the rules of the new game they are playing. They don't know that a spiritual war is on and that they have a new Enemy, who wants to kill and destroy them (see John 10:10; 1 Peter 5:8). They don't realize they need spiritual protection, nor do they know what weapons and armor are available to them or how to use them (see Ephesians 6:10-18). They need a disciple-maker who will be their shepherd.

Shepherds lead their sheep to water and make sure they have food to eat. They protect their sheep from wild animals and from those who would love to cut them away from the flock and lead them astray. If a sheep is missing, the shepherd goes looking for it. Jesus, the Good Shepherd, was a great protector of His little band of disciples. He did not lose any of them except for Judas, whose betrayal was a fulfillment of prophecy (see Psalm 41:9). In the garden of Gethsemane, Jesus protected the disciples so the soldiers would let them go (see John 18:7-8).

Likewise, as shepherds of God's sheep, disciple-makers must also protect the sheep in our care. That means if we are teaching a class or leading a small group, we should follow up with those who are absent and do our best to ensure that everyone in the class is present. It requires work and commitment to chase the strays, bind up the hurting, and lead and feed those we are shepherding. True disciple-makers do all we can to guide those we disciple to safety and maturity.

Of course, it would be impossible to do this kind of shepherding with a large group. I believe that this is why Jesus chose only twelve men to disciple. He was giving us a model of discipleship to follow, and He knew that in our finite state we could disciple only a certain number of people at a time. When a disciple-maker is responsible for shepherding more than twelve people, it is far more likely that some will fall through the cracks because there are just too many people to get know all of them well. And remember, if you don't know people, then you don't know where they're at and what they need in the spiritual growth process.

At Real Life this kind of shepherding happens in our small groups, which are a primary part of the relational environment we have created. However, small-group leaders are like everyone else. Their lives are filled with all kinds of stresses they have to deal with, including having to get ready for the next meeting's lesson. Consequently, they can neglect to make sure that they are growing themselves. They also can forget to make sure the disciples in their care are really okay. Small-group leaders can organize their lives in such a way that they have no ability to shepherd because they are just too busy. This turns their group into another transfer-of-information class—which leads to a loss of real discipleship. When we are too busy to be in relationship for real growth and we are not growing spiritually, it is time to change our lives.

When we first started Real Life, I got together with our developing leaders and we read Ezekiel 34:2-5 together. In this passage, God rebukes the shepherds of Israel for their lack of care for the people. The leaders had not brought back the strays or searched for the lost. They had accepted the title of shepherd because of all the privileges that came with it, but they did not take on the responsibilities that came with the title. So God cursed them.

Let's not be guilty of ignoring our responsibilities as shepherds. Sheep stray. People become hurt, are tempted, get distracted, and wander off. Intentional disciple-makers care enough to go after the spiritual infants and children God has brought into our lives.

Transparency

Transparent people don't pretend to be something they are not; they allow others to see them for who they really are. They are not hypocrites. They understand that we all struggle, so when they are struggling, they don't hide it. Who we see is who they are: the good, the bad, and the ugly.

Jesus was as transparent as He could be. He was not ashamed to show how He felt. He wept openly (see John 11:35). He got angry (see Mark 11:15-16). There are times when He was in emotional pain, and He told His disciples about it (see Mark 14:33-34; John 12:27). There are times when Jesus was discouraged and amazed at the hard hearts of men (see

Matthew 11:20; Mark 6:6; 8:21). I am sure He laughed. Right before He went to the Cross, He was afraid when He cried, "May this cup be taken from me" in the garden (see Matthew 26:39). Jesus was tempted in every way that we are, but He never gave into temptation (see Hebrews 4:15). He felt discouraged and challenged at times (see Matthew 17:17; John 12:36-37), but He kept on going. The Scriptures give us this encouragement: "Consider him who endured such opposition from sinners so that you will not grow weary and lose heart" (Hebrews 12:3).

Jesus' transparency served an important purpose in the disciple-making process. Throughout Jesus' life, He made it clear that following Him might cost someone his or her life (see Mark 8:34-35). He knew they were going to experience a wide array of emotions over their lifetimes. He didn't want them to have any illusions about how they were going to feel. We should desire the same for those we are discipling.

Believers are supposed to do the Christian life *together*. That is what it means to be a Christian, and that is especially what it means to be spiritually mature. When I am transparent with you about my struggles in circumstances and with sin, I am saying to you that I struggle too. I'm human too. I am saying that I trust you enough to share my inner battles with you and that you should do the same with another. Christians fail; we ask for forgiveness if we have wronged someone, we do our best to make things right, and then we move on.

When we are transparent about our struggles, we are taking them from the darkness, where the Enemy can distort them, and bringing them into the light. The Devil loves to tell us that we are justified in our sin because no one has it as hard as we do. He also loves to tell us we are so bad that we will lose everything if we tell others about a struggle — that people will leave us. He loves to tell believers that we are too unworthy or uneducated to share our faith. (He is called "the accuser of our brethren" [Revelation 12:10, NASB].) If he can convince us to hide our areas of struggle, he wins.

That is why James tells us to confess our sins to one another and be healed (see 5:16). When we confess our sins with other believers, we—and they—learn that everyone struggles. They discover that we all struggle with our sin nature. We all stumble in what we say, think, and do. We all live in a broken world that causes us pain. It is a part of the human condition.

Let me be clear. I am *not* saying that we should "show off" our sin so we can make others feel better about theirs. I *am* saying that if you and I spend any amount of time together, you *will* see me sin. To pretend for your sake that I do not have sin makes me a hypocrite and makes you feel that you have to be perfect as well. And none of us is going to be perfect.

It is very important that the leader of the small group creates this kind of authentic, safe environment. He or she sets the tone. I can't tell you how many times I have been open with fellow disciples about a personal struggle only to hear a huge sigh of relief from the group. Then they confess *their* struggles, and we can get down to business and deal with real things.

Again, this kind of transparency is not likely to happen in a large group. At Real Life we try to keep our small groups under twelve because people simply can't know each other "for real" in a larger group.

Accountability

Spiritual growth requires both authenticity and accountability. When people are transparent about their struggles, they need to be held accountable to live out the changes Jesus wants to make in their lives.

But disciple-makers must earn the right to hold others accountable. Therefore, at Real Life we encourage and help our small-group leaders earn the right to call the disciples on their mistakes. If we are loving shepherds, those we are discipling will know that we love them and care for their well-being and we will have credibility when we speak into their lives. Once transparency and authenticity have been developed, we can see what people really believe and how they really live. At that point, we can lovingly and courageously address the behaviors that do not glorify God and that hurt the person involved.

When someone is sharing a problem or concern, praise that person for sharing and make sure he or she knows we are all sinners. Then say something like "What can we do to help you with what you have shared?" If the person doesn't seem to want to change, back off for the time being and deal with it later.

When authenticity is a value in a group, some people will share their stuff simply because they want credit for being honest. They don't want to change, and when asked how the group or disciple-maker can help, they say in so many words, "Back off—don't judge me. At least I am being honest." When this happens, I often ask (in private), "I am glad you are being honest, but now what do we do with this?"

It's important to realize that some people don't want accountability. They would much rather surround themselves with folks who tell them what they want to hear. The Word tells us, however, that the wounds of a friend can be trusted (see Proverbs 27:6). It's valuable to have friends who care about us so much that they are willing to confront us for the glory of God and our own good. True friends tell the truth in love (see Ephesians 4:15). True friends stick beside us even when we fail, yes, but they also tell us what we need to hear and then help us accomplish what they tell us.

My life verses are Hebrews 3:12-13: "See to it, brothers and sisters, that none of you has a sinful, unbelieving heart that turns away from the living God. But encourage one another daily, as long as it is called 'Today', so that none of you may be hardened by sin's deceitfulness." The word *encourage* in this passage can mean to encourage, support, or exhort, but it can also mean to admonish. In other words, the Scriptures tell us to say to our friend, "Hey, what are you doing? Stop it!" or "Hey, get with it!" in a loving way. Notice also that these verses call us to do this relational support daily. God tells us through the Word that we need constant encouragement and correction to stay the course. The source of sin is deceitful, tricky, enticing. We are in a constant battle with our flesh, the culture, and the Enemy of our souls. I am reminded when I look at the statistics for Christians that there is a direct correlation between those who are going to church occasionally and the spiritual fruit, or lack thereof, produced. Those who are in a consistent relational environment for discipleship and support are experiencing transformation; those who are not, are not experiencing transformation.

Keep in mind that real relationship for discipleship is not one-sided. Accountability must be mutual. Leaders have not arrived at perfect spiritual maturity; we will make mistakes too, and we need to allow those in the group to hold us accountable when we are wrong. The Liar (see John 8:44) will entice us, and we need each other to keep from falling. James 5:19-20 says it this way: "My brothers and sisters, if one of you should wander from the truth and someone should bring that person back, remember this: Whoever turns a sinner from the error of their way will save them from death and cover over a multitude of sins." Mutual accountability creates a culture of genuine relationship that will then be a part of the lives of those we are discipling.

A word of caution: Be sure not to address every issue that needs to be dealt with in the life of a disciple all at once. I am so glad that God deals with things a little at a time in my life, and we must use that model in holding others accountable. If God showed me every one of my foibles and sins all at once, I would curl up in a ball on the floor and suck my thumb.

Guided Practice

Jesus was a great disciple-maker because He taught His disciples how to reproduce the discipleship process in others. During the time He was with the disciples, He always kept in mind the end goal. He wanted disciples who knew the truth, who were changed from the inside out, and who would have some very important skills. As they matured and developed spiritually, He allowed them to practice what He was teaching them.

Although I don't know this for sure, I think that initially Jesus' disciples acted as His bodyguards. (Yes, they were *big* fishermen.) Then they started collecting enough food to feed the five thousand and collect the leftover fish and bread (see Matthew 14:19-20). But He also gave them more complex assignments as they grew up: He sent them out by twos to minister (see Mark 6:7-12). When they returned from their mission, He debriefed them (see verses 30-31). And at the end of His earthly ministry, He sent them out to do what He had done with them (see Matthew 28:19-20).

Great disciple-makers will always take their followers through a process. It starts with "You watch; I do" and moves to "Let's do it together" and then to "You do; I watch." Finally, the disciple starts this same process with someone else — someone who watches while the disciple does.

At Real Life we go through this process with everyone, from the leadership team on down. For instance, most of our small-group leaders started out in a small group, where they learned and watched the small-group leader. Later they became apprentices to the small-group leader and co-led the small group. As apprentices they met with the leader on a weekly basis for debriefing and any needed training. Finally, they led a small group of their own. As small-group leaders, they usually met weekly with their coaches and monthly with their community pastor for debriefing and further training.

We've taken hundreds of small-group leaders through this process of guided practice. Some are still leading small groups, and others are now on the mission field, on staff, or maybe even planting a church of their own. However, everyone started at the same place, and their gifts and calling emerged as they were doing relationship for the purpose of discipleship. Everyone needs a place to practice what they are being taught.

Guided practice works best in a small group. Few people have the gifting to speak in front of thousands. But most of us feel okay speaking to a few people we are really getting to know. In a small group, we can develop skills that may give us the ability to speak in front of many more. Everyone needs a starting point, and a small group is the perfect place.

JUST ONE OF THREE KEYS

Do you remember the three keys to discipleship?

An intentional leader + relational environment + reproducible process = infinite number of disciples

Relationship by itself is not discipleship. Relationship is *a* key to discipleship, but having good friends, a good marriage, or a great small group in which everyone feels loved and accepted does not necessarily mean a person will mature and progress through the five stages of spiritual growth. Sitting in a small group, feeling all warm and cozy, and discussing our issues with each other is not discipleship any more than taking a Bible class or mastering theology is discipleship by itself.

We've discussed the roles of an intentional leader and a relational environment in the discipleship process. In the next chapter, we'll examine the third key: the reproducible process.

To learn more about discipleship at Real Life Ministries,
go to thestoryofreallife.com.

Chapter 5

STRATEGIC: FOLLOWING A REPRODUCIBLE PROCESS

Most wrestlers don't like basketball, so I hate to promote a basketball coach as an example of a great coach, but Duke University's Mike Krzyzewski fits the bill. He has taken his program to postseason play in twenty-five of his twenty-eight years at Duke and is the "winningest" active coach in NCAA Tournament play. To date, his Duke teams have won eleven ACC Championships, been to ten Final Fours, and won three NCAA Tournament National Championships.

Many of the teams he coaches against are led by men who once played for him or were one of his coaching assistants, including: Tommy Amaker (Seton Hall, Michigan, Harvard), Bob Bender (Washington), Mike Brey (Notre Dame), Jeff Capel III (VCU, Oklahoma), Johnny Dawkins (Stanford), David Henderson (Delaware), and Quin Snyder (Missouri, NBDL Austin Toros). Not only are these guys honorable men but they understand the game and have become great coaches as well.

So here is what I believe about great coaches. Many can get lucky once if they stumble on some great athletes. However, a great coach creates an intentional, repeatable system that consistently develops great players and leads to consistently great teams. Remember though, success is not just about winning; it is about creating players who become great men and eventually great leaders.

My point is this: A reproducible process enables the next generation of leaders to understand what to do and how to do it. Great coaches do not leave the process to chance.

Without question, Jesus was a master coach. When He told the apostles to make disciples, they understood what that meant. They knew what to do because of what He had done intentionally with them.

JESUS' REPRODUCIBLE PROCESS

Let's look at Jesus' process for discipleship. Over the years, our church sought to study the Gospels to discover Jesus' process for making disciples. Remember, we believe He was the greatest disciple-maker in history—He knew what He was doing. As we studied, we saw a pattern that was passed on to the early church. Our church has given it a name. We call it the Share, Connect, Minister, Disciple process (SCMD).

Jesus shared, connected, trained those who followed in ministry, and released disciples to make disciples. In the beginning of His earthly ministry, He extended His official invitation to Peter, John, and the others after a miraculous catch of fish (see Luke 5:1-11). The men in Peter and John's boats struggled to bring in the fish, almost sinking with the haul. Then with all that fish in front of them, Jesus told them to leave their livelihoods as fishermen and follow Him. (Jesus' goal was not to make their business successful but to show them who He was.) With this miracle, Jesus **shared** with His disciples the truth that He was the Messiah. Granted, the disciples weren't close to understanding all of this truth yet, but they had heard as much as they could handle, and they believed. At that point, Jesus extended an invitation—"Come with me"—or maybe better understood—"Come be with me."

Jesus, the disciple-maker, not only **shared** the truth about Himself with His disciples but also offered an opportunity for them to **connect** with Him. As I described earlier, over the next few years, He spent time training these men who would carry on the work of changing the world. During that time, He replaced their old ideas of reality with the truth. He taught them in a variety of ways as he created a relational environment by shepherding them, by being transparent, and by holding them accountable. As the disciples grew spiritually, Jesus gave them opportunities to put what they were learning into practice. This is how He trained them to **minister** to the people who came to hear Him. As they became more confident, He sent the disciples out by twos to preach and do miracles. When they returned, He took them to a place to rest and asked and answered questions (see Mark 6:30-32). When they got too cocky, He reminded them that they were to be servants and not lords (see Matthew 20:2-28). When they failed, He explained why. Jesus was the master of debriefing His disciples about the experiences they were having.

At the end of His time on earth, Jesus did what every good disciple-maker does. He sent His disciples out on their own (however, they were really not on their own since they had the Holy Spirit and each other) to make disciples themselves who could, in turn, make disciples themselves. Jesus successfully transformed His small group of followers from catchers of fish to catchers of people.

We can also see the SCMD reproducible process in the way the early church functioned.

SCMD IN THE EARLY CHURCH

The book of Acts begins with the disciples waiting in an upper room for the Holy Spirit to come. What happened next was amazing. The Spirit descended upon the disciples, and they began to preach with great power and conviction. Peter **shared** with thousands the truth he had come to accept, and those who accepted the message were baptized (see Acts 2:41). But the apostles didn't stop there. They had been taught differently. They knew that something had to come next, so they **connected** with the people who responded to the Pentecost message (see verse 42). All the believers met together daily in houses and in the temple courts. They were devoted to the fellowship, but they didn't just hang out together. Theirs was fellowship with a purpose. They were devoted to the apostles' teaching and to prayer (see verse 42). They remembered through Communion what Jesus had done for them.

These new believers had to learn a new way of looking at life. As Jews they had an understanding of the Old Testament, but they had been taught they could earn their salvation through good deeds, so they had much to learn and much to unlearn. This could happen only as they walked and talked with more mature believers.

As time went on, new converts were being added to their number, and it became more difficult to care for everyone (see 6:1-7). Eventually, it came to light that the Greek widows were not being taken care of adequately. At this point, the leaders in the early church did not do what many pastors would do today: either ignore the problem, saying they can't take care of everyone, or taking on the task themselves, believing it is their job to do everything. But the disciples knew their role, and they were determined to be organized in ways that would allow them to keep doing the specific work they had been given. They were given the task of spending time with God in prayer and teaching and organizing the believers. Because they understood that every believer had a position to play and that abilities given by the Spirit would enable them to do it, they evaluated the gifts and abilities of the believers in the church, looking for people who were filled with the Holy Spirit and were emerging servant leaders.

They chose seven men to step into the role of **minister** to these widows (see 6:5). In this role, these men learned what it meant to take care of people and were able to develop skills as they grew and matured. They were able to see spiritual needs and watch more mature believers serve. They learned what to do and what not to do. As they carried out the tasks of ministry, including some that seemed mundane, the disciples got to see and assess each man's character.

Sometimes believers will refuse to do a specific job, such as taking care of the physical needs of people, because they see it as being beneath them. They want a more "important" job. It is my belief that if a person will not do a simple, thankless task, he or she doesn't yet have the character for a more visible position.

Of the seven men who were chosen, two stand out: Stephen and

Philip. Stephen stands out because he became the first martyr in Jerusalem. A persecution broke out as a result, and the church was scattered. Philip, who had been a servant to widows, became a preacher in Samaria, a culturally and geographically place distinct from the work in Jerusalem. Someone had shared with Philip, and he entered a **connect** environment. He then became a **minister**, serving food to widows. Finally, he became a **disciple** who could reproduce this same intentional process with others in Samaria.

Throughout the first centuries, the members of the early church reproduced the SCMD process in others. For example, Saul became Paul with the help of Barnabas (see Acts 11:22-26). Barnabas went on to disciple Mark and others (see 15:36-37). Paul later discipled Titus (see Titus 1:4), Timothy (see 1 Timothy 1:2), Luke (see Colossians 4:14), and Silas (see Acts 15:40), along with many others. Paul told Timothy, "The things you have heard me say in the presence of many witnesses entrust to reliable people who will also be qualified to teach others" (2 Timothy 2:2). Paul had taken him through a process that he charged Timothy to reproduce with others.

The believers in the early church knew they were supposed to make converts (who were baptized) and make disciples (who were able to reproduce). These disciple-makers were intentional; they knew how to be intentional in a relational environment, living out a process that could be followed by others.

Let me close this chapter by telling you a story that shows how this process works in the lives of believers at Real Life.

SCMD AT REAL LIFE

Kelly is a well-known country-music singer in our area who came to the Lord about four years ago. He owned the largest country-western bar in the region. He accepted Christ while listening to a financial tape series that was created by a Christian. The man who shared the series with Kelly didn't follow up with him in any way, so this spiritual infant had to figure out the rest on his own. As he began to read the Bible and pray, something strange started to happen to him. He came to know that he could not continue doing what he had done before—he needed to close the bar. After struggling with the decision for some time, he finally made the move. The people in our town didn't know why Kelly had done it; some thought he must be going to Nashville.

Not long after he shut things down, he began to wonder what his real purpose was. He had time but little direction. He was unconnected and floundering a bit when a friend invited him to church. He hadn't been to a church and wasn't sure he wanted to start, but eventually he gave in and came. The service that weekend lit him up because it was about what a Christian is saved from and for: a Christian's God-given purpose. He began coming on a regular basis. Not long after that, I met him in the foyer and invited him to my small group. In that group the guys took him under their wing and began to invest in him spiritually as well as relationally. Previously Kelly had no Christian friends, so we all did a lot of hanging out. Over the next months he changed so much, and as he grew, he began to tell everyone what the Lord was doing for him.

Before long he got the old band together to create a Christian country-music CD. Because he was still very popular in our area, the bars invited him to play. Soon he began to travel all over the country. Most people he sang for had frequented his bar before he sold it, so they asked him why he had done so. He gladly shared with them about Jesus and all that He has done in his life. Now when Kelly performs, he sings some old secular tunes mixed with his new Christian music; then he shares his testimony and closes by singing "Amazing Grace." Not what most would expect in a bar, but it has led to incredible things.

As he grew, he continued to share with his band members, who had noticed a huge change in him—obviously. As he lived out his faith and shared it with all who would listen, people responded. He invited them to church and many came. He also became a small-group apprentice in a men's small group (while still coming to ours), and he continued to grow as he **ministered** in very simple ways.

About a year after he started in our small group, Kelly had another life-changing moment as he ministered through his music and around our area. A guy in his band whom Kelly had known for years asked what in the world had happened to him, and Kelly **shared** about Jesus. Sure, this guy had heard Kelly talk about it many times, but after seeing real, consistent change in Kelly's life, he was ready to listen. The guy said, "I want that kind of peace. Can you answer some questions for me?" Kelly said that he would try. When his friend started asking his questions, Kelly knew he was in over his head and said, "I want to take you to my pastor, and he will answer the questions for you." The man replied, "No offense, but you are my pastor. I don't know that guy. I know you—you answer me." Kelly told him he didn't know the answers to his questions but that he would find out. So Kelly told our small group he had a list of questions he needed answers for.

When he told us the story, I knew his life was about to change again. Kelly was about to learn what it means to grow up and become a spiritual parent. He was going to help a spiritually dead person have a saving relationship with God. He was then going to help that new infant grow up as he had been growing up. He was **connecting** with him, and with our help he knew what to do next. Our small group and I invested in Kelly, and he invested in another. Now Kelly leads his own small group, and the guy he won to the Lord is, after two years, starting his own group as well (**disciple**).

The SCMD reproducible process works when implemented in tandem with an intentional leader and a relational environment.

For more tips and tools for discipleship,
go to reallifediscipleship.com.

Part 2

MASTERING THE
DISCIPLESHIP PROCESS

Chapter 6

ONLY OUR PART

Before we go any further, I want to make sure that you understand your part in the spiritual growth process in the lives of the people you are discipling. First, we must remember that those we disciple are really disciples of Jesus—not of us. They must imitate us only as we imitate Christ. Second, as disciple-makers we play a part in the process and we are responsible to do things Jesus' way; however, young disciple-makers, and even experienced ones, can forget they are not solely responsible for the failure—or success—of those they disciple. It's easy to take too much blame or too much credit for the results, or lack thereof. This either leads to pride and stealing glory from God, or it leads to discouragement. Always remember that God is the primary agent of salvation and change in a person's life.

GOD'S PART, OUR PART, THEIR PART

There are three important pieces in every situation where God would use us. First, God Himself is working. He precedes us in seeing a person's heart and knowing the need. He is the One who changes hearts. Second, we are a tool in His hands. We ask God to help us see opportunities and make the most of them by sharing, connecting, training for ministry, and the releasing of disciples. Third, the person God is working on must respond to Him and to us.

So often we think we are a failure because we witnessed to someone or encouraged someone to obey God and he or she did not respond.

As disciple-makers, we need to remember that we cannot do God's part, nor can we do the other person's part. We can do only our part.

The Bible makes it clear that no one comes to the Lord unless drawn by Him (see John 6:44). Our job as believers is to do what Paul outlines in Colossians 4:2-6:

> *Devote yourselves to prayer, being watchful and thankful. And pray for us, too, that God may open a door for our message, so that we may proclaim the mystery of Christ, for which I am in chains. Pray that I may proclaim it clearly, as I should. Be wise in the way you act toward outsiders; make the most of every opportunity. Let your conversation be always full of grace, seasoned with salt, so that you may know how to answer everyone.*

Our job is to pray that God will act and then to watch for Him to do so. God is drawing people to Himself, and He will use us if we will allow Him to. He is the Great Chess Master, and He can bring His pieces into position so that He can use them.

In the Colossians passage, Paul also says that our attitude is to be one of thankfulness—joy, peace, and contentment. Oftentimes believers are seen as "doom and gloomers" instead of people with peace. Paul also tells us to be wise. The book of James tells us what godly wisdom looks like. "The wisdom that comes from heaven is first of all pure; then peace loving, considerate, submissive, full of mercy and good fruit, impartial and sincere" (3:17). Wisdom is peace-loving and considerate, full of mercy. Christians who are always looking for a fight are not wise. Christians who are not full of mercy are not wise.

James tells us to pray and live wisely among outsiders (as the Bible describes wisdom) and to make the most of every opportunity when it presents itself. Opportunities most often show themselves in the form of a need we notice in the lives of those around us. Notice that living wisely and prayer both precede the opportunity. God is at work in people's hearts, and He is the one who brings them across our path.

It's our job to recognize the opportunity and to respond. We are not responsible for whether a person accepts the message; that responsibility lies solely with the individual. I recently had to remind one of our small-group leaders about this truth.

A REAL-LIFE STORY

Years ago Chris had had an affair and nearly lost his wife and family. Through that experience, he and his wife came to Christ and their marriage was saved. About a year ago, they felt led to start a small group for couples whose problems involved unfaithfulness in the relationship. Three of the couples in the group did well and their marriages were on the mend. However, one couple had continued to struggle and was on the verge of divorce.

Chris came to my office one day, discouraged and feeling like a failure. I asked him what he had done to try to help. He said he'd called them, met with them, studied the Scriptures with them, advised them to see a counselor, and made an appointment for them with a pastor. On and on it went.

"Chris, so you are telling me you are a failure because *their* marriage is in trouble?"

He said, "I feel like I must have done something wrong."

I explained the three parts I have just described: our role, God's role, and their role. I asked him to tell me what he had noticed that God had done in this couple's lives. He said God had spoken through His Word, He was living in them, and He was working on them. God had sent people to try to help them.

When I asked if Chris and his wife had done what the Bible tells them to do as shepherds for these people, he said he wasn't sure. So we went through some Scriptures outlining what Christians are to do for one another. Chris said that he had done all those things.

"Chris, it sounds as if God has been doing His part and you have been doing your part. So what is the problem here?"

He replied, "I guess they are not doing their part."

"Chris, you and your wife were faced with the same decisions this couple has to face if they want to save their marriage. You made those decisions, and the result has been amazing. Is God willing to do for them what He did for you?"

Chris knew that God was.

"Did you have someone come alongside you to help when you were going through your situation?"

"No. We tried to get help, but we couldn't afford a counselor, and the pastor at the church we were attending was too busy."

"So God worked and you worked even though you had no help?"

"Yes."

"In the case of this family in your small group, God has been working and you have been working. These people have more opportunity to save their marriage than you had, but they won't step up, right?"

Once again, Chris replied, "Yes."

"Then you cannot take responsibility for their actions; you can only do your part. You can pray for them and love them, but you cannot fix the marriage for them. It is their choice."

WHY PEOPLE DON'T RESPOND

I don't want to imply that sometimes we can't learn to do things better. We can. But there are a number of possible reasons for why a person might not respond positively to the gospel message or to our encouragement or correction. In the case of a witnessing opportunity with a lost person, perhaps we were trying to force something on the person that God was not in on. I don't mean that God wants anyone to be lost; He doesn't. But He knows each person's heart. Perhaps we are only one of several messengers of the gospel message and it will take several people's efforts before the person receives Christ. Or it could be that God is working in a person's heart or life, but the person we are sharing with is choosing not to respond.

We see this in the story of the rich young ruler. One day a rich young man come to Jesus and asked how he could inherit eternal life (see Matthew 19:16-22). Jesus didn't always respond to every person the same way. He had the advantage of knowing exactly what was in every person's heart. In this case He put His finger right on the problem. Jesus responded to the man's question with truth and love, telling him that he had to sell everything he had and follow Jesus. What happened? The young man didn't respond to the offer to become a disciple of Jesus. He wanted to keep what he had, even though what he had clearly wasn't enough. (If it would have been enough, he wouldn't have come looking for what was missing.) The rich young man chose to keep what he knew and what he was comfortable with rather than follow the Lord Jesus. Had Jesus failed because the man didn't follow? Had He done His part perfectly? I hope you know the answer to those questions. Someday God will meet him and say, "You are without excuse. I spoke to you and you would not respond."

God is not dependent on our perfection to win someone He is working on. Nor is He dependent on us to disciple someone perfectly. That is where we go wrong. We forget that the people we disciple are not *our* disciples; they are *Jesus'*. He will never quit working on them. We can't do God's part. We can't do the other person's part. We can only do our part.

For more real-life stories about discipleship,
go to thestoryofreallife.com.

Chapter 7

MOVING THE SPIRITUALLY DEAD TOWARD LIFE: *SHARE*

Remember the stages of the spiritual growth wheel? Let's look at it again.

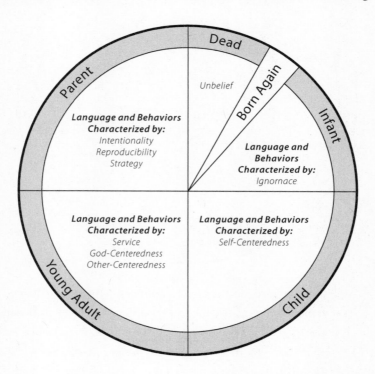

Every person is born into this world spiritually dead. Those who receive Jesus are born again. The Holy Spirit moves in and they become spiritual infants. As they grow and mature, they move from the infant stage to the child stage, to the young adult stage, and finally to the parent stage, in which they disciple someone else through these same stages.

To better understand how the SCMD process relates to the different stages of spiritual growth, look at the outer ring in the following chart:

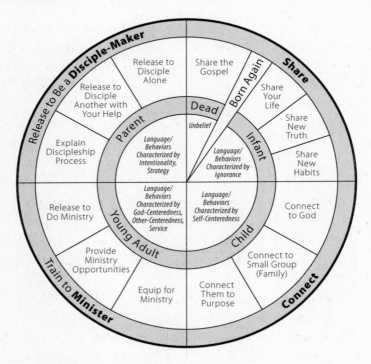

Note that I have added the Share, Connect, Minister, Disciple process to the stages of growth we first talked about in chapter 3. The chart works like this: The inner circle describes the stages of spiritual growth with key characteristics that can help a disciple-maker assess where people are at spiritually. (Remember that people will reveal where they are by what they say and do. The "phrase from the stage" tells the disciple-maker where to start in the process of discipleship.) The outer circle shows the reproducible discipleship process and how it aligns with the spiritual growth stages.

In the rest of this chapter, we'll look at how to **share** with a person who is spiritually dead. (In the next chapter, we'll look at how to **share** once this person has been born again and become a spiritual infant.)

RECOGNIZING THE SPIRITUALLY DEAD

As I stated in chapter 3, the spiritually dead are characterized by their unbelief in Christ, which shows up in various ways, such as a rebellious attitude toward God. Because the sinful nature is allowed to rule in the heart of the spiritually dead, the relationships of an unbeliever tend to be shallow or broken.

The beliefs, values, attitudes, and behaviors of the spiritually dead include:

- Disbelief in the supernatural, or belief in many forms of the supernatural (multiple deities, interactions with the dead, superstitions, astrology, and so on)
- Disbelief in God (atheism) or belief in the possibility of God (agnosticism) or belief in a God that is different from the God of Scripture
- Belief in one God but many ways to get to Him
- Anger toward Christians or the church
- Ignorance and or confusion about God, Jesus, and the church
- Misinformed about spiritual/biblical truth; spiritual blindness
- Belief that the answers they are seeking lie in worldly prestige, power, fame, and so on
- A belief that they are as good as anyone else, so they don't need a Savior
- A belief that they have done too much wrong and a fear that they can't be saved
- A belief that what is right for you is right for you and what is

right for another is right for him or her; there is no absolute truth — right or wrong

Some of the representative things the spiritually dead say (the phrase from the stage) that reveal who they are include:

- "I don't believe there is a God."
- "The Bible is just a bunch of myths."
- "I don't believe in miracles."
- "Evolution explains away a need for God."
- "God is just a crutch."
- "I am not a Christian because Christians are responsible for all the wars in history."
- "There are many ways to get to God."
- "I don't need to be saved since I am as good as anyone else."
- "A good person gets to go to heaven and a bad person goes to hell."
- "I believe in heaven, but there is no hell."
- "I am a Christian because I go to church and I am a good person."
- "There is no hell because God is a God of love."
- "I have been a good person, so I will be okay."
- "It doesn't matter what you believe as long as you are sincere."
- "There is no absolute right and wrong."
- "I don't know where I am going if I die."
- "I believe in Jesus, but my friend is a Mormon. I told her it didn't really matter as long as we believed in Jesus."

UNDERSTANDING THE NEEDS OF THE SPIRITUALLY DEAD

Remember that every person is unique. Some people have been raised with a non-Christian worldview, such as Buddhism or Hinduism. Others doubt God's existence. Still others are from Christian homes where they saw a lot of inconsistency; they believe in God but don't like the church or Christianity. Despite the differences in their backgrounds, the needs of the spiritually dead are simple. Some of the things they need include:

- A secure relationship with a mature believer
- A picture of the real Jesus lived out in front of them
- Answers, evidences for Christianity, and answers to life's hard questions
- An explanation of the gospel message
- An invitation to receive Christ

If we are to share our faith with the spiritually dead, we must build an ongoing relationship with them. As we do, we will discover their reasons for not being a Christian if we listen well. We must earn the right to speak into their lives so that we can deal with these issues one at a time. The best evidence for our faith is the kind of love we give to others.

As we begin to share our faith, we won't always be able to answer the questions that are raised, perhaps because we don't have the knowledge yet or we don't think the way that specific unbeliever thinks. We may never have struggled with that person's particular doubts or questions (although we have struggled with our own), so we must be humble enough to say, "I don't know, but I will find out. Let's meet next week to talk about it." All good disciple-makers don't start out ready; we become ready as we start out. By scheduling a time to meet again the following week, we also strengthen the relationship. Remember not to allow the only reason you meet with someone to be his or her conversion. The person will pick up on this and feel like he or she is just an objective to be reached—a person to be converted. The relationship isn't real and often people will see through that.

I have interacted with many people in this stage. I spend time with them and give them information to read and listen to that will challenge their thinking about spiritual things. I give them material and expect them to do some of the work because I want to gauge their willingness to search. This tells me how serious they are about learning about Christianity. If they won't do any of the heavy lifting, it usually means they are not ready. While many I have met with have come to know Christ, others have not. Some people just like to argue, but I have found that we can not argue anyone into the faith. That does not mean I don't continue my relationship with them, it just means I keep earning the right to speak into their lives, and I keep praying that God will do what He needs to do to open the door to their hearts.

Here is a short list of topics that many unbelievers wrestle with:

- How a good God could allow the evil that happens in the world
- The authority of Scripture
- Evolution — Is there a God?
- The violent parts of church history, such as when Christians killed the Muslims and others
- Atheism and agnosticism
- Previous hurts from past involvement in the church
- Cults
- What makes the Bible different from other religious books

(If you would like to study some of these issues further so that you are better able to discuss them with the spiritually dead, see the list of recommended resources in appendix B.)

While the spiritually dead need answers, the answers that mean the most to them are the ones that come from a changed person. Seeing Christianity work as it is designed to work in the lives of others can bring a person around in ways that a book or information never will.

I have noticed that many people reject Jesus because of what they *think* Jesus said rather than because of what He actually said. For example, I can't tell you how many times I have heard people say they can't be a Christian because God hates homosexuals or because Christianity promotes bigotry. But the Bible clearly teaches that God loves everyone and wants to save all of us (see John 3:16). He may hate sin but He loves people. Other folks are opposed to Christianity because of Christians who "laid down the law" with them but have not explained the context or the reasons *why* God has said what He has said. The spiritually dead need to understand that everything God commands is for our good, for our protection. It is true that His rules are His rules, but understanding His heart behind those rules can change everything. Of course, some people will not care why God has said what He has said in His Word. They just don't agree, and there is nothing more we can do except love and pray for them and wait for their worldview to come crashing down around their ears. We cannot change the Bible in order to make it more palatable to someone.

Our culture is constantly attacking the Christian faith. Whether it is a college or high school teacher, the History Channel, or a work of fiction, such as *The DaVinci Code*, challenges to the authority of the Word come from every direction. There are good and reliable answers for all of the challenges, and disciple-makers need to know where to find them so that we can address spiritual questions and concerns when they come up.

WHAT TO DO WITH THE SPIRITUALLY DEAD

Share Your Testimony

Disciple-makers need to be able to tell others who they are and what God has done in their lives. The spiritually dead need to hear about our experiences with God. We must be truthful and be sure not to sound as though we are perfect, because those we spend time with will soon discover our foibles anyway. As we share, we can talk about how God has changed us and made us less of a mess than we were.

We should also be careful not say that God will do something in the life of a saved person that His Word does not clearly promise. Time and again, Christians promise that when we come to Christ, God will take away our problems and make everything okay—that He'll make us wealthy or healthy and so on. But Jesus doesn't promise these things. Yes, He works in our lives, and our lives change. As believers, we are less likely to make choices that hurt ourselves or others. And yes, God does bless us; He walks with us through our troubles. However, Christians still have problems, and sometimes coming to faith in Christ brings new problems. New believers now have a spiritual Enemy, and some will alienate family and friends by choosing to follow Jesus. So let's not attempt to win nonbelievers with false promises.

All Christians struggle, and people need to know that. If they come to Christ for the wrong reasons, then when life doesn't go as they think it should, they will walk away from Jesus disappointed. Or they will think they must have done something wrong and that God hasn't saved them because they are too evil. If we act as if we're always on fire for Jesus and they know they are not, they will think something is really wrong with them.

Earn the Right to Share Christ

As I mentioned earlier, we earn the right to share Christ by the way we act. By loving people, we earn the right to be heard. For instance, maybe someone gets sick in your office and you make a meal and take it to his or her house. Or maybe you show up at the hospital. Perhaps you remember a birthday. Or when you hurt someone, go to that person and say you are sorry. Most people are not used to hearing that. When they see that we are different, they open the door of relationship and we can share Christ with them.

I have often heard from unbelievers that they want nothing to do with Jesus or the church. When I ask why, they tell me that churches are for Republicans and that they are Democrats. What this tells me is that Christians are often better known for who we vote for on earth than for who we live for in eternity. Some believers are more interested in their rights as outlined in the Constitution than in giving up their rights as Jesus did so that people can be saved. These "political" Christians have the bumper sticker that says, "My boss is a Jewish carpenter," next to another one that says, "I'll give you my gun when you take it from my cold, dead hands" — or something like that. Sadly, these messengers are getting in the way of the message.

Don't misunderstand me. We need to stand against things that are contrary to the things of God. But make no mistake: We should not fight like the Devil for the things of God! The Scriptures tell us to be prepared with an answer "when we are asked" about our faith and to answer with gentleness and respect (see 1 Peter 3:15). Notice that our faith is to be evident enough that people will ask us about it. We don't shove it down their throats. And we certainly are not to be like a clanging cymbal, making sure everyone knows they are going to hell.

Pray That God Shows You Opportunities to Share

Pray, *Lord, help me do what You want me to do and to say what You want me to say.* It's critical that you pray every day for God to help you see what He sees. Allow His Word to wash you spiritually. John 17:17-19 tells us that we are sanctified by His Word — that His Word is truth. Ask Him to help you care about what He cares about. When this is your prayer, He will help you be aware of what is happening around you spiritually, and He will give you the wisdom to know when and how to respond.

For example, I have been on many plane rides, and in talking with the person next to me, I've become aware of an opportunity to share my faith. I don't know if I will ever see the person again, so I say, "Would you like to hear what I believe about that?" I will then go as far as the person will let me. I don't want to be pushy, but I believe that the Lord has me there for a reason.

When God uses us to bring someone to Christ in one of these unique short-term circumstances, we must make sure the person knows about his or her need for a spiritual parent and family. Get a phone number or e-mail address so you can follow up. Use the Internet to search for a good church near the person's home and then let him or her know what needs to happen next. We do what we can in these situations, remembering that's all we can do. God will do His part.

Share the Gospel

This is a difficult task for most. Yet even the newest of Christians can and should witness to a spiritually dead person. (See appendix C for a list of spiritual facts to share with those who are spiritually dead.)

Within a few years after their conversion, many Christians have converted most of their unbelieving friends. Those they have not converted have usually disassociated themselves because they don't want to hear about Jesus anymore. As the new believer has grown, his or her interests have changed and the friendship has cooled. Some new believers didn't try to convert their friends at all and now hang out only with other believers because they need the support and don't want to be with people who will draw them to their old lifestyle. However it happens, many Christians don't associate much with those who don't yet know Christ.

While I understand the decision to be careful about whom we have for our closest friends, as we grow in our faith, we must become intentional about being around unbelievers. How else can we become disciple-makers? We need to make an effort to stay in spheres of influence where non-Christians gather, whether it be at our children's baseball games or the neighborhood garage sale or the company picnic. Our mission is not to play it safe but to take ground from the Enemy.

The Devil repeatedly tells growing believers that we are not good enough to share the gospel or that we don't know enough — that we need to be able to answer deep theological questions before we can share our faith. But if the Lord has *you* in a relationship that leads to a spiritual conversation (and He will lead you there), and *you* don't know the answer to a question the person is asking, then that question must not be the real or whole problem. Perhaps He is leading you into the relationship so that you can learn more about the question and provide answers in this situation, or for a future opportunity. At Real Life we teach our people to say this when they don't know the answer to a question they've been asked: "I will have an answer in another week; in the meantime let me tell you what I do know, which is what Jesus has done in my life."

Please understand that I am not saying there is no need to get ready to be a good witness. We *should* study so that we can answer hard questions, which is why I've included a list of resources at the back of the book. But even those who don't know the Bible well yet can talk about what God has done for them personally. The Holy Spirit gives us the words the person really needs. Remember, we cannot argue anyone to the faith. If someone wants to fight, love that person. Answers won't bring a fighter to the kingdom anyway.

While we must be prepared to ask people if they want to give their hearts to Jesus, remember a one-time visit usually doesn't do it. Sometimes we get to close the "deal," so to speak, because God has been working on them and using others as well, and other times we simply say or do something that makes the person think. Perhaps we just set the stage for another Christian to bring the person to Christ. Just remember that God is drawing this person to Himself and He has brought you into his or her life. He knows what He is doing. Trust Him and give all that you have.

It has been our goal at Real Life to equip people to be able to do the job God has given them to do, so we put together a card that can help Christians share the gospel. I have included it in appendix D for you to copy and use. Whether you use it or another evangelism tool, don't bypass learning and practicing this skill, particularly if you are a pastor or church leader.

EVEN THE PASTOR NEEDS TO PERSONALLY SHARE THE GOSPEL

A few weeks ago, one of our staff leaders was asked to come to a church to help them determine why there had not been a single decision for Christ in over a year. He sat down with three of their church staff and asked, "Have any of you ever personally won anyone to the Lord?"

They of course said that they had, so he asked them to get their Bibles and, each one at a time, take ten minutes to share the gospel with him as if they were talking with a friend who had never heard about salvation through Jesus. The senior pastor paused, then stammered, then finally got quiet. He put his head down and said that he didn't know how to share the gospel on a personal, one-on-one level like that. He confessed that because he knew how to preach, he just asked people to fill out a card or maybe come down the aisle for prayer after the message. But he had never won anyone to the Lord outside of a church service. Besides all that, he spent most of his time working with Christians and hadn't spent much time with unbelievers anymore. It was a very honest moment.

This explains why his congregation had had no conversions. This pastor didn't know how to witness, so his people were not equipped to do it either. He had not created a culture of one-on-one evangelism. He had merely created a service and hoped that the people at his church invited their friends. Of course, decisions have been made over the years in this kind of system, but God's plan is to release an equipped Spirit-filled army on the world. The worship service is a support to the active believers; it is not the main evangelistic tool. Again, true conversions seldom happen because of a church service alone. Oh, some pastors can really "wow" people and get them spiritually hyped up for a short time, but it often wears off because there is little support. Decisions for Christ, if they are real and sustainable, are made because the Holy Spirit has already been working in that person's life through an individual. To be a disciple-maker, we must be able to effectively share our faith one on one, and then support the growth we see God accomplishing—pastors included.

See appendix C for more about how we continue to share once a person has accepted Christ as Savior.

Chapter 8

NURTURING SPIRITUAL INFANTS: *SHARE*

God designed Christianity to spread across the earth like the common cold: through contact. He intended for us to share our faith with others and then disciple those who decide to follow Jesus. If all conversions happened in that way, we would clearly know when a person makes a decision to follow Jesus; it would be easier to know when we are dealing with spiritual infants, and then we could start the process of investing in their spiritual growth. However, many people hear the gospel, believe it, and then are left to sort through the Christian life on their own. The result? Spiritually immature people representing Jesus to the world. When the majority of Christians are immature in their faith, is it any wonder few want to be Christians? Most believers haven't changed much and don't have much information to share.

For the disciple-maker, the critical questions are: Who are spiritual infants? What are their needs? How do I disciple them?

RECOGNIZING SPIRITUAL INFANTS

Spiritual infants are characterized by their ignorance, confusion, and dependence. They have accepted Jesus as Savior and Lord, but they still don't know much about what it means to be a Christian. They are in the honeymoon stage of their walk with God. They are often excited about their faith and can become very zealous for Jesus, but they are just beginning to be changed by Christ (this is called "sanctification").

Because the Bible plays a part in a person's being changed and new believers usually know little about the Bible, they don't change much at first. They might be fired up and want to know Jesus more, but they are often naive and vulnerable.

Here's a case in point. Tom serves in our church as a small-group leader and a security person during events and services. I met him years ago when one of our home group leaders, Sam, asked if I would come to his workplace to meet with one of his employees. Sam had been witnessing to Tom and bringing him to church and to his home group, and Tom wanted to meet me.

Sam told me that he felt Tom was ready to make a decision and that his live-in girlfriend was also ready to accept Christ. However, the girlfriend feared that Tom would end the relationship if she put a stop to their sex life and demanded that they get married. Sam said she was ready to end the relationship if necessary but was hoping that we could get through to Tom.

When I got to their workplace, Tom and I talked for an hour about Jesus. He made it clear he believed in Christ and was ready to make a commitment, so we prayed together and then planned his baptism. After we had dealt with the real issue — salvation — I asked Tom, "Is it true that you are living with your girlfriend?"

He said that he was, and he excitedly told me that his girlfriend was ready to accept Jesus too. (He didn't know we had already spoken with her.)

"Are you aware of what the Bible says about sex before marriage?"

He paused for a moment. "No — what?" I could hear the angst in his voice, as if maybe he had just been ambushed.

I explained that Jesus said fornication was sin and that no follower of His would purposely live that way. I will never forget what Tom said next.

He threw his hands in the air in an animated gesture. In a shocked voice he said, "Why? Why would God say that? You have got to be kidding!"

Because he was a spiritual infant, Tom had never heard of such a thing. For the next hour, I showed him what Jesus had to say about sex outside of marriage (for example, see 1 Corinthians 5:9; 1 Corinthians 6:9, Galatians 5:16-19; Ephesians 5:3). At the end of the discussion, Tom looked at the table, dejected. He said he didn't know if he could handle life without sex, and he didn't know if his girlfriend could handle it if they stopped sleeping together either. He loved her, but he didn't know if she would marry him.

I said, "The first real issue is this: Are you willing to put Jesus first? Is He going to be your Lord or not?"

"Yes, no matter what."

"Then you need to go home and talk to your girlfriend."

Sam and I knew that Tom was in for a pleasant surprise. We left elated, though Tom left with much fear and trepidation. He was a spiritual infant who was a part of a family. He had accepted Christ. His spiritual parents had just helped him take a step in his growth process. Later the home group leader helped Tom and his girlfriend live separately until they could get married. Many nights Tom talked with his leader about how hard it was to keep his hands off his future wife. Many nights they prayed through his struggles and talked about what God says about marriage. Not long after that, they were married. Over the years, Tom grew and is now a leader who has joined his spiritual parents as a co-laborer.

Can you imagine what would have happened to Tom if Sam hadn't been working with him and I hadn't gotten a chance to sit with him and deal with real issues? What would have happened if he was converted and then left to fend for himself? I believe he would have gotten stuck in the baby stage of spiritual development for years, if not forever.

While Tom is an example of a spiritual infant who had little Bible knowledge when we met, other spiritual infants have a ton of Bible knowledge from listening to many sermons, but they grow little because no one guides them through the process of growth. These Christians remain spiritual infants because they miss the point of the gospel: relationship with God that leads to relationships with others (see Matthew 23:24). I believe that most American Christians are stuck in this stage because they were converted and then allowed to stay in the nursery.

When spiritual infants stick around long enough to become a part of the church culture, they can pick up the Christian lingo and eventually mimic the behaviors of more mature believers—at least while they are in public. When this is the case, there is little substance or depth behind their words and actions. They will do the "right" things—they will look mature—but for the wrong reasons. As soon as life gets tough—and it will—infants will wither away. Until then, the church becomes a pageant, a place to put on the "perfect" face so that they look like everyone else. But inside, their lives are rather empty.

The beliefs, values, attitudes, and behaviors of spiritual infants include the following:

- Ignorance about what they need spiritually and what the Bible says about life and the purpose of a Christian
- Ignorance about or frustration toward Christianity and the church
- Belief that Christians make no mistakes; unrealistic expectations of themselves and others
- A belief that they are defined as the culture would define them
- A worldly perspective about life with some spiritual truth mixed in
- Mixing some of Christianity with some of other religions but not knowing it

Some of the representative things they may say (the phrase from the stage) that reveal who they are include:

- "I believe in Jesus, but my church is when I'm in the woods."
- "I don't have to go to church to be a Christian."

- "I gave my life to Jesus and I go to church, but I don't need to be close to other people."
- "I don't have time to be in relationship with another Christian."
- "My spouse is my accountability partner; I don't need anyone else."
- "I pray and read my Bible; that is good enough for me."
- "My ministry is my secular work; I don't have time for the church."
- "I didn't know the Bible said that."
- "We were born as spirit children in heaven before we were born down here as humans, correct?"

MEETING THE NEEDS OF THE SPIRITUAL INFANT

Spiritual infants need:

- Individual attention from a spiritual parent
- Protection and care
- To have the Word of God explained to them
- To have the habits of a believer explained and modeled

Spiritual infants need protection and care in order to grow up into mature spiritual adults who in turn disciple others. They need a spiritual parent to **share their lives** with them so that they see the substance behind our words and actions and to correct their misperceptions and be authentic with them. (A relational environment is important for real learning, which is why **share** overlaps a bit with **connect** in the discipleship process.) However, don't expect infants to seek something they know nothing about; they need us to invest in them.

They see people at church smiling all the time, so they mistakenly think all Christians are happy and have few problems. When they hurt, they think there must be something wrong with them.

Spiritual infants need spiritual teaching because by themselves they won't get much right in their spiritual lives. Others, because of their success and experience in the world, are extremely disciplined and think that if they can make themselves do the right things on the outside, that means they are spiritually mature. The result? They become prideful. The inside—their character—hasn't matured because no one has challenged their motives. Pride begins to separate them from everyone in their lives. They also do not understand that by receiving Christ they have just become an enemy of the Devil and that they need to put on the spiritual armor (see Ephesians 6:10-17) that God provides. The job of the disciple-maker is to explain what happens when someone is born into the family of God and what will happen next.

WHAT TO DO WITH SPIRITUAL INFANTS

The bottom line is this: Spiritual infants can get stuck without a spiritual parent to move them beyond their faulty perceptions and keep them from traveling down dangerous paths. Disciple-makers must create a relational environment so the spiritual infants in our care can continue to grow and learn as we share our lives with them. In so doing, we teach them new truth and help them develop appropriate new habits as Christians.

What truths do disciple-makers need to teach spiritual infants?

Teach them about the spiritual battle that surrounds them. New believers are not aware that we are in a spiritual battle. I often use the movie *The Matrix* to explain this concept to a new believer. (There is much I disagree with in this movie, but it is helpful as long as I point out my differences with it as I use it.) Most people have seen this movie, so it is something that new believers can understand.

The main character in *The Matrix* is Neo, a young computer genius and technology pirate who has come to understand that something is wrong with the world. In the beginning of the movie, he doesn't know what's wrong, but he intuitively senses that something's amiss.

He has heard the legend of Morpheus, a person who has found the answers many seek. Unexpectedly, Morpheus comes to Neo to offer him a chance to know the truth. Morpheus warns Neo that all he offers is the truth—good or bad as it may be—just the truth. Neo chooses truth, and it opens up a whole new world to him.

As Neo sees the real world for the first time, he begins to understand that the human race is living in a computer-generated lie, and they are captives to evil alien programmers who are using the human race for their own evil purposes. All the while, the oblivious human race believes they are really living a normal life. Morpheus and his small band of followers have the task of teaching Neo the new rules in the real world (a great picture of discipleship) so he can play his special part on the team that has been given the mission of saving the human race. Freeing people proves incredibly difficult because most people who are stuck in the matrix have no interest in being freed. In the movie, there are evil agents trying to protect the false world the computer has generated. They can show up anywhere, anytime, and they will stop at nothing to keep Neo and the rest of the team from their rescue mission.

Again, *The Matrix* is not a perfect parallel to the Christian experience, but it does help new believers who come from our modern culture understand the spiritual battle we are engaged in. Christians have the knowledge of the truth and must learn to work and live in it. Our job is to reach those still enslaved to the world's system. When someone chooses to live in the light of the truth, we must teach that new believer to live as part of God's team. We also have enemies in the spiritual realm who will stop at nothing to continue to deceive and manipulate the human race. Of course, we have the Word of God, God's manual for life, and we have the Holy Spirit guiding us.

You might feel more comfortable using something other than *The Matrix* to explain the reality of the spiritual battle. That's fine. I am more interested in helping you develop a game plan for discipling others than in giving you a curriculum to master. What's important is that you explain this truth to the spiritual infants in your care and do so in a way they can understand.

Teach them how spiritual transformation works in our lives. Disciple-makers also need to help spiritual infants understand they are on a journey. Though they will not understand *all* the ways they eventually need to change, they need some direction about which way to head. They not only need to know what now, they need to know what's next. They need to know that the Devil will try to get them to doubt who God is and who they are as His children.

I usually share this truth with new believers by helping them understand the difference between two theological terms, *justification* and *sanctification*. Without this understanding, spiritual infants can doubt their salvation when they fail, and they will certainly fail. So to explain these theological truths, I use a white robe and a red robe and a small bucket of mud. I either draw them (I am a bad artist) or use actual robes and say something such as the following.

When we are physically born, we enter the world with a sinful nature that will show itself soon enough. We are born as cute, innocent babies, but deep inside us is a disease that will reveal itself: We are born with a propensity to sin. If I use the robes, I put the white robe on the young disciple and explain that each of us is born into the world as an infant. As we grow up, we put hands in mud (sin) and wipe it all over ourselves. Every time we sin in thought or in deed, it's a new mark. Because I don't usually carry around mud and robes, I go through the motions as well as draw it on paper.

God sees our sin, even if others don't, and because He is holy and perfect, our sin separates us from Him. In comparison to a perfect God, we are a mess (even if we are not as dirty as someone else around us), and it is His perfection and standards by which we will be judged. Sin is rebellion against God, and we have all chosen to rebel against Him and His ways. We have chosen to be our own king rather than let God be ruler of the world He created for us. This is sin: a willful act of disobedience. The Bible teaches that the wages of sin is death. We are all dead spiritually (see Romans 6:23). However, Jesus came to give us a way out.

Next I draw a cross with the red robe draped on it and explain that when we come to the cross, we can put our sin-stained robe on the cross (I share that Jesus actually put that dirty robe on and paid for it on the cross) and exchange it for the red robe, which we then put on. The red robe represents Christ's blood that was shed for us. It represents the perfection and righteousness Jesus lived out in His earthly life. Jesus takes on our sin and gives us His righteousness. If we accept Him as our Messiah, our Savior and Lord, He gives us His righteousness because He took on our sinfulness. We are now *justified* (given His righteousness) by His grace through our faith. When God sees us now, He sees Jesus and declares us justified and righteous — clean.

Once we are saved, the Holy Spirit who once worked *on* us (by drawing us to God [see John 6:44]) now works *in* us. Though we wear the robe of Christ, when we look under the red robe, we still see our sinful nature and bad attitudes. Though we are "declared righteous," we still struggle against sin, but the Holy Spirit is changing us from within so that our outside starts to look more like what we have been declared to be. He is transforming us to be like Christ. That is the process of *sanctification*, and it lasts until our sinful nature is finally destroyed in heaven.

As Paul tells us in Galatians 5:16-17, this isn't a pain-free process; we have a war going on within us:

> *Walk by the Spirit, and you will not gratify the desires of the flesh. For the flesh desires what is contrary to the Spirit, and the Spirit what is contrary to the flesh. They are in conflict with each other, so that you are not to do whatever you want.*

Paul makes it clear that we are experiencing inner turmoil as believers. New believers need to understand that this internal struggle is part of the transformation process. The fact that they are experiencing an internal war and are aware of their sinfulness and hate it is evidence that they are Christians (rather than evidence that they are not). Yet their internal struggle can lead them to worship. When we understand that Jesus has saved us in spite of our wickedness and that we are no longer held captive to our sinful nature, His grace becomes breathtaking. The bottom line is this: When God looks at us, He sees that we by faith are covered by the blood of Christ. He has also sent the Holy Spirit to change us. We are becoming on the inside more and more like what we were declared to be on the outside. We are completely justified and are in the process of being sanctified.

Teach them about the stages of spiritual growth and the discipleship process. To do this, I go over the information on the chart entitled the Summary and Profile of Each Stage of Spiritual Growth in appendix A. I also explain the stages of development and the role of the disciple-maker, or spiritual parent. Remember, they don't understand the rules of the game, so to speak, and this is a great time to explain why they need a guide (disciple-maker).

Teach them what new habits they need to develop. Every year when I coached, I always had a parent and new-wrestler orientation meeting, where I made sure the wrestlers and their parents knew what was ahead, what it would cost to be part of the team, and what they could expect in return. For instance, I told them they would have to develop some new habits. I expected them to get up early and run two to three miles a day because wrestling takes incredible endurance. I expected them to commit to keeping their body pure — no drugs or alcohol — and to be careful about what they ate. I expected them to lift weights three times a week. I told them that they had to be at practices or they couldn't compete for the school in dual meets. I told them that if they did these things over time, their bodies would change shape and they would become the toughest men on the campus. Their commitment to training and discipline would affect everything they did; they would be successful in life because they would learn discipline and commitment. Every year some of the kids would quit after that meeting. Sometimes the parents themselves would say, "No way." Many of those who stuck it out became honorable young men who developed character.

In the same way, new believers need to understand what a Christian should look like and what habits to develop in order to grow. I teach that Christians:

- **Need a personal Bible study plan or method.** We are people of the Word because it is through the Word that we are sanctified — purified. The Word helps us know right from wrong. Through it, we are able to defend ourselves spiritually.
- **Meet together and are a part of the church.** Christians are devoted to meeting together. The early church did this on the first day of the week and daily. I share with them the components of the weekend services (music/worship, communion, offering, etc.) and why we do it. They will feel like they have joined a club and don't understand any of the language if you don't explain things.
- **Serve others.** We use our gifts and abilities (which God created us with) to serve individually and corporately for the glory of God.
- **Pray.** We pray for others, and they know it.
- **Give to others.** We want God's glory and the good of others more than we want the things of this world. We are people who tithe our income and resources and give even over and above.
- **Are in relationship.** We are committed to our marriages and families. Our marriages and kids are more important than our careers. If we are unmarried, we are committed to sexual purity. We are committed to other believers. We look past others' faults, we forgive, and we seek forgiveness.
- **Are humble.** We know that God created us with our abilities. We know that He also spiritually gifted us with ways we can serve. We are merely managers of those gifts and we use them

for His glory. We also know that we are sinners and it is only by the grace of God that we are not in hell. Therefore we want to give others the same grace that God has given us.

- **Share our faith with all who will listen.** We do this even if people persecute us for doing so. People are going to hell without Christ, and we love people best by giving them what they need, not what they want.

This lifestyle may be strange for new believers, which is why we must help them understand the *what* and the *why* of discipleship. God has given us His guidelines for our own good and His glory. He loves us, and just as a good parent sets the rules for their children's good, God does the same.

A WORD OF ENCOURAGEMENT

I know that many reading this are recognizing that they are not as spiritually developed or prepared as they thought they were. If that's you, you might question whether you are capable of discipling someone else. If so, the following analogy might help you understand what you can do.

Imagine for a minute that my son is eight years old and has been hanging out with his friend down the street. As he is walking home one evening, he hears a whimper coming from the grassy roadside. He walks over and sees a baby lying in the grass, hidden from passing cars. What if my son said, "Wow, a baby!" and then thinks, *I am too young to care for a baby*, and walks on home? Did he do the best thing for that baby? The loving thing? The responsible thing? Would I be proud of him? Absolutely not. While my son is not old enough to parent a baby, he is old enough to know that a baby needs a parent and to pick it up and bring it home so it can get the care it needs, either through our family or another family.

In the same way, you may not be ready to care for a spiritual infant or child, but you are able to recognize when parenting is needed. At Real Life we encourage everyone in our church to be a member of a small group, and we encourage those who are young in their faith to bring those they have shared with (or other spiritual babies they find along the road) to the group so that they can be cared for by more mature believers. You can do the same.

Keep in mind that in order for a family (small group) to care for a spiritual infant, there needs to be at least a spiritual young adult leading the group. If a spiritual infant is thrown into a small group with only other spiritual kids who are not prepared to care for an infant, then that infant will obviously not be cared for or raised properly. He or she will possibly die or at best grow up with some seriously bad habits. A young adult can at least babysit on the short term, much like my wife and I would bring in a teenager to watch our toddlers when we went out on a date night. Disciple-makers need to be sure that spiritual infants are protected and cared for by someone responsible and knowledgeable enough to guide them to maturity.

For more tips and tools for discipleship,
go to reallifediscipleship.com.

Chapter 9

GUIDING SPIRITUAL CHILDREN: *CONNECT*

Sunday mornings at our church are crazy. We have so many people and so many back-to-back services that children's ministry check-in and checkout can be nuts. Sometimes mothers come in frazzled and late. We are careful with our kids, so we have some stringent precautions and processes parents must go through when dropping off and picking up their children. Sometimes things can get a little heated because the parents want to get into the service in order to find a seat, or they had a bad morning at home, or whatever.

One Sunday a volunteer worker came to one of our children's ministry leaders after the early service and announced, "I am done!" The dialog between the leader and the volunteer went something like this.

Leader: "Are you okay? What happened?"

"This parent became frustrated because it was taking too long to check in her child and she yelled at me. I lost it. I told her that she couldn't treat me that way. I'm a volunteer. I didn't sign up for this!"

Leader: "I'm sorry. You're right; they shouldn't have yelled at you for doing your job to protect our kids. But can I ask you, why did you volunteer for the children's ministry?"

"Because the leader at our small group told us that there was a need in the children's ministry. Everyone at the group that night just signed up."

Leader: "Why did *you* sign up?"

"Because everyone else did."

Leader: "What did you think would happen if you helped out?"

"I thought it would make me feel good to serve and that I would be appreciated."

When the leader asked the volunteer if they could start meeting, the volunteer declined, saying, "I am too busy to meet with you, and I won't be helping anymore anyway."

This volunteer had accepted Jesus as Lord and Savior. Someone had helped her **connect** with a small group, and she was actively involved in it. She knew she was to play a part in the church. Some people might assume that this woman was a spiritual young adult because she was serving the church, but her answers to the leader's questions revealed that her motivation for doing so was that of a spiritual child.

Spiritual children are significantly different from spiritual infants. Although spiritual infants are ignorant and typically see Christianity in "just me and God" terms or "me, God, and my spiritual parent" terms, spiritual children are actively engaged in some type of small group for discipleship. They have made a basic commitment to **connection** with a spiritual family, which is good, but they need more. They will even take on ministry tasks, but their reason for doing so is often not the result of a changed heart. For them it is about being part of the club. It is about getting something for their efforts. Spiritual children need individual attention if they are to become a spiritual parent someday.

Let's examine how we can recognize spiritual children, what their needs are, and how to disciple them.

RECOGNIZING SPIRITUAL CHILDREN

Spiritual children are young in the faith yet have grown in many ways. They are learning how to understand biblical concepts and can speak using biblical terms. The Word of God is becoming their road map for life, and their habits and priorities are changing. However, they still are prone to doing the right things for the wrong reasons. They often do the right thing conditionally—as long as it leads to the right destination as they have determined it. They are often characterized by attitudes such as self-centeredness, idealism (if I give the right thing, I will get the right thing), the two extremes of pride, or a low view of their value to God. They are often controlled by their emotions so they are up and down.

It can be challenging to determine where an adult Christian is at in the spiritual growth process. With children, you can estimate their age based on their size, but spiritual age and maturity aren't so obvious. There are other difficulties as well. When it comes to spiritual maturity, the number of years someone has been a Christian doesn't matter. Some of the most spiritually immature people I have ever met have been in the church for sixty years or more. Conversely, some of the most spiritually mature people are young people who have been Christians for just a few years.

This is one reason why at Real Life we developed a system to help us accurately assess which stage of development a person is in. (Adults might take offense at being called a spiritual child, which is why it is important to help believers understand the spiritual stages that all disciples go through and to clarify that spiritual children are not less valuable in God's kingdom than spiritual parents are.) Again, we know a tree by its fruit, and out of the overflow of the heart the mouth speaks. Most anyone can sound mature for a while, but over time we see who that person really is. This is why relationship is a needed part of discipleship. Our job as disciple-makers is to know what a spiritually mature person looks like and then do our part to guide those in our care into spiritual maturity.

The possible beliefs, values, attitudes, and behaviors of spiritual children include:

- Excitement over having deep relationships, which they might not have had before
- Remembering who they were as unbelievers so they appreciate how God has changed them
- Understanding much of the Christian language

- Disillusionment because of their high expectations of others
- Belief that feelings are most important, which leads to spiritual highs and lows
- Lack of wisdom about how to use what they are learning—for example, too aggressive when sharing their faith or too legalistic in their approach to dealing with their friends and family
- Belief that people are not caring for them enough
- Mimicking mature Christians' behaviors in order to look good and gain praise
- Serving others in a ministry as long as the benefit outweighs the cost
- Enthusiasm about new teachings
- Confusion and being black-and-white on complex issues because they have an incomplete view of biblical subjects
- Knowing more about what Christians say than about what the Word says

When we ask spiritual children where they got a particular view they hold, they often quote a Christian teacher rather than God's Word. In contrast, mature believers test what they hear from others and know the Word. They are not easy to fool. They know the voice of the Master, and they won't follow another. Not so with children.

Some representative things spiritual children may say (the phrase from the stage) that reveal who they are include:

- "I love my small group; don't add any more people to it."
- "Who are all these people coming to my church? Tell them to go somewhere else!"
- "I am not coming to church anymore. It has become too big; it has too many people."
- "My small group is not taking care of my needs."
- "I don't have anyone who is spending enough time with me; no one is discipling me."

•"I didn't like the music today. If only they did it like . . ."

•"I am not being fed in my church, so I am going to a church that meets my needs better."

Notice what word is used in each of these phrases: *I*. Believers at this stage often talk in terms of *I* because they are focused on their own perceived needs and opinions. They have not progressed to the point that they have become servants of others; they still believe that the world revolves around them.

Spiritual children are spiritually immature for a variety of reasons. Some are newer believers, and even though they have progressed quickly and with intention, they still have far to go. Others have been saved for years but have never **connected** in a relational environment for discipleship, so they sputter along with just one cylinder hitting. Perhaps they were involved in a church but had little investment from an intentional leader (parent) because there wasn't one to be had or because they didn't want one. Again, some spiritual children have been Christians for years and have a lot of Bible knowledge and years of church involvement but inside remain immature. They have decided to follow Jesus at the head level, but their heart and hands are not engaged.

Here are some additional ways spiritual children reveal their spiritual immaturity.

They believe things about life and faith that are biblically inaccurate. This is because they have an incomplete view of Scripture or truth. They have not had mature believers challenge their perspectives and their practical application in ways that would give them a more complete view. They are naive because ministry or service is not often about black-and-white theological issues. Service brings maturity. Paul explains this as he tells leaders to equip the saints for works of service so that the body might be built up (see Ephesians 4). He then speaks of the maturity that comes from this equipping and service and adds that adequately equipped believers "will no longer be infants, tossed back and forth by the waves, and blown here and there by every wind of teaching and by the cunning and craftiness of people in their deceitful scheming" (verse 14). In other words, spiritual children are tossed to and fro by different doctrines.

This happens because they have not been firmly rooted in the truth and have not gained the experience that can come only through service and relationship with others. They are like the newly trained student teacher who has studied the books for four years and understands teaching at just the theory level. The individual is about to learn the hard way that actually teaching students is different than talking about teaching students. Knowing the content is only half the battle.

They do the right things but for the wrong reasons. As disciple-makers, we must look at the motivation of disciples who want to serve. Jesus made it clear that people can say or do the right things but have hearts that are wrong: "These people honor me with their lips, but their hearts are far from me" (Matthew 15:8). The following story illustrates what Jesus was talking about.

Our small group was learning the story from Luke 5, where Jesus tells His disciples to leave their fishing nets to come and follow Him. My apprentice pointed out that Jesus said that if we gain our life, we will lose it, and if we lose it, we will gain it. When I asked the group what that meant, Will shared that when he became a Christian, he had to give up chasing the world's approval. He had worked hard and neglected his family for years because he felt he had to prove to his dad and the world that he wasn't a loser. When he became a believer, he started to work at the things that mattered most, and his life became much more satisfying.

As Will spoke, Steve was squirming. Steve had just retired from the military. His wife had tried for years to get him to come to church, but he thought church was for "wusses." I met him at a football game because our kids were on the same team. When I invited him to church, he told me he would come *once*. About a month later, Steve came to a worship service, and that day his heart started to change. About two months later, he accepted Christ and was baptized. He started coming to the small group I was leading and was growing like crazy.

When Will finished, I could tell that he had struck a nerve in Steve, so I asked what he was thinking. Steve said, "I need to get busy and do something in the church."

My wife, Lori, looked at him intently as he spoke, and then out of nowhere she asked, "Why, Steve? Why do you need to get busy and do something?" She was picking up something I had missed. I recognized that look on her face.

"I just feel I need to do something more for God."

Lori continued, "Why do you feel you need to do something more?" As she prodded, Steve opened up, and we discovered that he felt he needed to do more to be saved.

Think about that for a minute. What if we had allowed Steve to serve in a ministry—perhaps made him a small-group leader or a youth sponsor? He would have been serving in an important job with the wrong motivation. His purpose would have been to earn something that he had already been freely given. He would have been directing whatever group he was leading to a "works" perspective on salvation. His cry would have been "Do more for Jesus so you can be sure you are saved!" He could have affected a great many people with his influence—and believe me, Steve earns influence fast.

Instead, because he was in a group with a good spiritual leader (my wife, in this case), this tragedy was averted. Lori had picked up something in Steve's comments that could have been seen only in relationship. No one would have picked up on his motivation if one Sunday morning during worship service he had simply responded to a survey about serving in the church.

After Steve's comments, our small group changed its focus to learning what saves us and what we do because we are saved. Steve was not yet ready to lead others. He was still a spiritual child and needed to remain in connection with the family in order to learn. He was not mature enough to be a leader in the church—yet.

Their service is conditional. Once again, children are self-centered. Some serve in order to earn spiritual points. Others, such as the nursery volunteer at the beginning of this chapter, like how serving makes them feel; they serve as long as the plusses outweigh the minuses. Serving makes them feel they are part of the club. They get something from it. But when reality sets in (and it surely will), they realize that to serve may cost them something, and then they are often gone. They don't mind being a servant as long as they are not treated like one.

Paul describes people like this in 1 Corinthians 3:1-3, where he says, "I could not address you as people who live by the Spirit but as people who are still worldly—mere infants in Christ. I gave you milk, not solid food, for you were not yet ready for it. Indeed, you are still not ready. You are still worldly. For since there is jealousy and quarreling among you, are you not worldly? Are you not acting like mere humans?" Though these folks were in a church (which at that time was comprised of small groups), they were still children or infants in the faith.

Before I move on, I want to clarify that I believe that spiritual children should be able to serve in minor ways in the church. After all, in the physical world we give our kids chores; we try to teach them to have a servant's heart and to be a responsible contributor to the family. However, there is a difference between allowing children the opportunity to serve and making them a leader. Before they lead, they must first learn to follow. They need to have a safe place to serve—safe for them and safe for the church body as well.

Sometimes spiritual children think that menial tasks are beneath them, particularly if they are successful in their work life. When that's the case, a spiritual parent must show them that humility is up and pride is down in the upside-down world they have accepted in Christ. Until we pick up a mop, stack chairs, or clean toilets—without praise and for the glory of God and the good of others—we have not learned what it means to serve Jesus instead of self. God is glorified when leaders are not above any task in the church.

We must know people well enough to know what is real in their lives, or there is the potential for a huge problem. Some spiritual children have great leadership skills, and we need to be careful not to misread natural ability for spiritual readiness. The better the natural leader, the more probable the potential problem. If skilled spiritual children are good in relationship building and can gain influence quickly, they will gain a following. And when spiritual children gain a following, they can do much damage to the family of God. They don't mean to be "bad." They often don't see that they are wrong; they are just trying to help. It's just that manipulation is the way of the world, and they are used to figuring out how to win and then proceeding down that path.

They are sophomores. Those at this stage of spiritual development have often learned what the Bible says about whatever topic they are interested in or whatever situation they may be dealing with. They can use a concordance and look up truths topically. They have heard some great sermons and are on fire for God's Word. They may know that adultery is wrong and can prove it from Scripture, but when it comes to how to respond to someone who is in adultery, they may not handle the situation as Jesus would have them. I call them sophomores because the word means "wise fools." They are wise enough to know the truth but foolish about how to use it. As a result they can be too zealous and push people away from God. They may see someone in the church gossiping, so they pull out Matthew 18 and come in with guns blazing. They use Scripture without understanding the intent behind it, and they have not learned to come with a right heart in love seeking reconciliation. They often read scripture about how the church *should* be and then get disappointed when it doesn't act that way in reality. They can be idealistic and naive. They allow few gray areas, even where perhaps there should be, and they can often become legalistic.

MEETING THE NEEDS OF SPIRITUAL CHILDREN

Spiritual children need teaching about:

- Being part of a spiritual family
- Feeding themselves

- Who they are in Christ
- Having relationship with Christ
- Having relationship with other believers
- Appropriate expectations concerning other believers
- Giftedness and what part the Lord has prepared them to play in the body of Christ
- Timing (just because they have leadership skill sets doesn't mean they are ready to lead)

Again, the rules of the game change when we enter into life with Christ. In the physical world, first is first and first is best. The one who has the most servants wins. But in the spiritual life we have inherited through Christ, last is first. In the old life, taking was the norm—get while the getting is good. In this new life, giving is the goal. In the old life, getting as much we can—*now*—is what mattered. In our new life, storing up treasure in heaven is the important thing. On and on it goes. Spiritual children need help learning how to live in this new life. That is what discipleship is all about.

At Real Life we prefer (although it isn't always the case) that spiritual children be connected to a spiritual parent (rather than a spiritual young adult) as their leader. A parent understands the components necessary for spiritual growth. We also encourage them to be connected to a small group focused on discipleship.

Some might assume that if a spiritual child is part of any small group at a church that he or she is in a **connect** environment and will grow spiritually. This is not necessarily so, as small groups can have different purposes. Some meet to do a task. For instance, our church has a small group where people meet together to knit blankets for the new mothers in the church. Although this group is a great ministry, the knitting circle is not a small group for the purpose of discipleship. However, it could become one if, while knitting, the women encouraged one another in their faith, studied the Word together, were honest with one another about where they struggled, prayed for one another, and held each other accountable. If the group sought out anyone who was missing, then it would be on its way to being a connect-level discipleship group. If the leader intentionally strives to develop these women so that they could later disciple others, then the group has the kind of connect environment that a spiritual child needs to mature.

We have other small groups that meet as a prayer group or a Bible study group. While these may appear to qualify as a connect environment, that is not necessarily the case. The same rules apply. Prayer alone or Bible studies alone do not make disciples. Many Christians would say they are connected, but when we describe what biblical discipleship looks like, they realize that their connections fall short of it. So often we use the same words, but they mean different things to each of us. When that happens, discipleship loses the power it has to transform lives.

A great example of a connect environment can be found in Acts 2. We have already talked about this, but I want to return to it here for just a moment.

> *Those who accepted his message were baptized, and about three thousand were added to their number that day. They devoted themselves to the apostles' teaching and to fellowship, to the breaking of bread and to prayer. Everyone was filled with awe at the many wonders and signs performed by the apostles. All the believers were together and had everything in common. They sold property and possessions to give to anyone who had need. Every day they continued to meet together in the temple courts. They broke bread in their homes and ate together with glad and sincere hearts, praising God and enjoying the favor of all the people. And the Lord added to their number daily those who were being saved. (verses 41-47)*

Note that the believers were devoted to and characterized by certain behaviors. Above all, they were committed to the Scriptures and to the apostles' teaching. We cannot grow spiritually if the Word is not central in our lives. The early disciples were also committed to taking Communion, remembering who they were and what God had done to save them. They spent time praying. Without prayer we cannot maintain a relationship with God; the disciples knew they needed to teach people to pray as the Lord had taught them to pray.

Read back over the passage and note all the relational words: *fellowship*, *together*, *in common*. The early disciples were a spiritually intertwined family, and they enjoyed spending time together. They ate together, which means that they spent time together socially. The groups had purpose: They shared and ministered to all who had need. No wonder the early church grew. Who wouldn't want to be a part of a group of people who acted that way?

WHAT TO DO WITH SPIRITUAL CHILDREN

Once we understand who spiritual children are and what they need, we must ask what these disciples need to know (head), be (hearts), and do (hands) to become mature believers. What do they need at this stage of their journey? If they have been in church for years and yet remain spiritually immature, we must help them move the information they already know in their heads to their heart and then to their hands. If they are new to the faith, we must help them grow in all three areas. So where do we begin?

What follows is a broad game plan for discipling spiritual children. This plan is not exhaustive, but it provides a place to start. Remember that relationship is the conduit by which these things can be taught and applied in the right way.

Give Them a Solid Biblical Foundation (Head)

Remember, discipleship always starts with the *head*. What *should* every Christian understand? Those who have grown up in the church often do not understand how little the rest of the world knows about what we believe. The Enemy has so distorted biblical truth that the unsaved often think they know what Christians believe, but they don't. In addition, many Christians do not understand the Bible well themselves. If truth be told, far too many believers have a hodgepodge of beliefs they think are Christian but are not. It's the disciple-makers' job to understand the starting point of those we are discipling and to begin at their beginning. Even if they have heard the beginning before, go through the fundamentals again.

The goal is to teach what is appropriate for that person at his or her stage of development and to use words he or she will understand. For example, spiritual children might find Revelation an interesting book, but its content is not as important to their spiritual growth as other books would be at this point.

Okay, now for an overview of what spiritual children need to know first. You'll notice that I've broken down the list of subjects using coaching terminology. I in no way mean to downplay who God is or make light of the subjects. This is simply a way to help disciple-makers understand their role. You might not talk about these areas in the same way I do or use the same illustrations. That's fine. The subjects to cover are what is important, not the details.

UNDERSTANDING THE GAME WE ARE ENGAGED IN

The Two Opponents

Team #1: God — the Father, Son, and Holy Spirit — One God in Three Persons

- God is all-powerful, all-knowing, everywhere present, just, righteous, holy, loving.
- God is the creator of everything (except sin).

Team #2: God's Opponent — Our Spiritual Enemy

- Satan is a created being, a fallen angel.
- He rebelled against God because he wanted to be God.
- He was cast down to the earth.
- He is powerful (more powerful than humans) and deceptive — a tempter, a murderer, an enemy.

- He has limited power—he is not all-powerful, all-knowing, or omnipresent.
- He hates God and wants to destroy His family (and team), the church.
- He is always trying to redefine God.
- He desires to destroy the souls of those God loves
- He fights against God's team to stop them from taking territory from him.
- He has captured the world to do his will.

The Game Board and Pieces

The World — The Playing Field
- How did humanity get here?
- How did the world get the way it is now?
- What is God going to do with it in the end?

Eternal Life — The Prize
- The moment this world ends, when Jesus returns or we physically die, we will live in eternal relationship with God in heaven or we will live eternally separated from Him in a place created for Satan and his angels, called hell.
- God is the judge of our eternal destination.

People — The Players
- People are created in the image of God, created to be in relationship with Him. We are given a choice to live in relationship with God or to live independently of Him.
- People are created to live eternally from the moment of conception; we are more than just physical bodies.
- If we sin, we are separated from God because He cannot be in relationship with those who are rebellious and unholy. This separation equals spiritual death. Why? Because to be separated from God, who is life, equals death. We experience a physical death and a second death spiritually.
- Everyone has sinned; therefore everyone will die.

- Because of sin, we are separated from God and from one another.
- We have a sin nature that is selfish and corrupt.

The Rescue Mission

- God the Father sent God the Son to reveal His heart to a lost and confused world.
- God will save and bring home those who choose to obey Him rather than live in rebellion against Him.
- God sent His Son to come and pay the sin debt that we owed. He will do so if we put our trust in Him and allow Him to pay what we owe.
- To be rescued, we need to believe that Jesus is God's Son and trust what He says about salvation. Following Him as Lord gives us access back into the family of God.

The Christian Is:

- At peace with God because we allowed Jesus to take our place and pay for our sin
- A part of the kingdom of God because we accepted Jesus as our King
- Justified by grace through faith
- Clothed in Christ
- Being sanctified, becoming holy (set apart for God's purposes) and righteous
- A child of God in the family of God
- Able to receive all the benefits of children of God
- Filled with the Spirit and guided by the Word
- Committed to discipleship and growing into a mature believer in Christ
- A disciple (a follower of Christ, one who is being changed by Christ, one who is committed to the mission of Christ)

Our Team

- God's church is the team we play on.
- Because we walk in the light (in relationship with Christ), we have fellowship with one another (see 1 John 1:5-7).

- We worship together, love and serve one another, and work together to complete the mission of Christ to save the world.
- Everyone plays a position on the team that he or she is uniquely shaped to fill and gifted to play.
- The team can do more together than individual members can do alone.
- The components of a worship service include singing, Communion, and offering.
- Many of those who were supposed to be God's representatives did not care enough to do the job they were given and have since gone AWOL.
- Some of God's team members have spent so much time fighting each other that they've never hit the field.
- All Christians struggle with their sin nature and must offer forgiveness and ask for forgiveness from others.
- Every Christian must have appropriate expectations of other people and of themselves.

The Directions: The Bible

- The Bible was written by men who were under the supernatural guidance of the Holy Spirit. It has been protected by God and is infallible.
- It explains all the rules, characters, pieces, and goals in the game.

The Strategy

- God loves people and wants to save them even though they rejected Him.
- Everything God has done He has for our good and His own glory, but the people who live in the world are deceived by the Devil and their own foolishness and do not know this.
- God the Son came from heaven to reveal the heart of God in person through Jesus Christ many years ago. Many in our world have not accepted this reality because they have not heard the message, do not have sufficient evidence for the message, or are

rebellious and don't want Jesus to lead them.

- The whole team has become a part of God's rescue mission to bring the message of His salvation to humanity.
- We are to go out and share this message and disciple (train up) all those who decide to receive Jesus as their Lord and Savior.

As disciple-makers, we want to teach the new truths. But we also want to help those truths find a place in young disciples' hearts.

From Head to Heart

God doesn't want us just going through the motions; He is pleased when what we do comes from a changed heart. Spiritual children are changed when they come to the realization that Jesus came to save them after all they have done. When the Holy Spirit makes His home in their hearts, they start to be changed at the core of their beings. They start to see people differently. Paul says it this way: "Christ's love compels us, because we are convinced that one died for all, and therefore all died. And he died for all, that those who live should no longer live for themselves but for him who died for them and was raised again" (2 Corinthians 5:14-15).

As spiritual children come to understand the truth of the Bible and spend time with Jesus, the way they look at themselves and others changes. They no longer refuse to honor God, and they no longer honor Him with only their lips (which is just as bad as refusing to honor Him). God has taken their old, hard hearts and given them new, soft ones.

What is the disciple-maker's part in this transformation process? To teach what it means to be a follower of Jesus and to show what kind of person God wants us to be. We need to teach *and* model spiritual transformation and help those we disciple connect to other believers who can also serve as models.

Here are the topics I cover in order to do this and some of the key passages of Scripture that address the topics. As before, this is not an exhaustive list but simply a starting point.

WHERE DOES CHANGE COME FROM?

The Word—God's Part in Our Spiritual Transformation
- Psalms 119:9,105
- John 17:17
- Hebrews 4:12

The Holy Spirit's Part in Our Spiritual Transformation
- John 15:1-6
- Philippians 2:13
- Galatians 5:22-23

Our Part in Our Spiritual Transformation
- 2 Peter 1:7
- Galatians 5:25
- Romans 12:1-2

The Part of Other Believers in Our Spiritual Transformation
- 2 Timothy 2:2
- Titus 2:4
- Proverbs 24:6
- Proverbs 27:12
- Hebrews 3:12-13

What Does a Christian Look Like?
- Galatians 5:22
- John 13:35
- 1 Corinthians 13:1-4
- Ephesians 4:1-4
- Ephesians 4:17
- Philippians 2:1-11
- Hebrews 11

What Is a Christian Committed To?
- Philippians 3:8-10
- 2 Corinthians 5:18
- Matthew 28:16-20
- Galatians 6:1

- 2 Timothy 2:4
- Hebrews 10:25

From Heart to Hands

What should spiritual children be taught to do with their hands? Remember, being a Christian is not just about knowing truth and being in relationship with God and others; it is also about *doing*—actively engaging in the mission of Christ on earth. Just as good parents train their kids to be adults who can take care of themselves and their future families, spiritual parents develop disciples who can function on their own someday. Keep in mind that this does not mean that a Christian can reach the point where he or she no longer needs the support, guidance, and accountability of other believers. Until we get to heaven, we will always need these things.

What follows is a list of things a spiritual child needs to learn to do.

Handling the Word of God Correctly

How to:

- Use the Bible correctly when confronted with temptation, as illustrated by Jesus (see Matthew 4:1-11)
- Feed themselves— "Man shall not live on bread alone" (Luke 4:4)
- Interpret the Bible accurately
- Fight with the Sword (God's Word)

Dealing with Other Believers Appropriately

How to:

- Deal with conflict
- Give wise counsel
- Hold someone accountable
- Accept criticism

Discerning God's Will

How to:
- Hear God's voice
- Make wise decisions

Play Your Part in Your Family

How to:
- Become the spiritual leader at home
- Become a team with your spouse
- Become a godly parent
- Become a support for your spouse

Witnessing to the Lost

How to:
- Give your testimony
- Invite someone into God's family
- Find answers for difficult questions

Being Involved in the Local Church

How to:
- Become a member of the church you are involved in
- Find out how to use your abilities and gifts
- Understand how the church works

So let's sum this up: Spiritual children have accepted Jesus as Lord and Savior and need a connection to a small group that will teach them about this new life in Christ. They need a spiritual parent who will teach them what they need to know about the Christian life and what Christians believe.

Chapter 10

TRAINING YOUNG ADULTS: *MINISTER*

The journey from spiritual infant to parent is filled with ups and downs. Disciples will often take one step forward and two steps back. They may even get disgruntled when the Lord pushes them in areas that they did not want to be pushed. This was true for a couple who came to see me not long ago.

Months earlier they had left our church, and now they wanted to talk. At one point they were leading one of our small groups because in our eyes they had become spiritual young adults and were on their way to adulthood with a little more investment. However, while leading the group, they began to experience some problems with their finances and jobs. The stress on their marriage became an issue, and we asked them to step back and just attend a small group while they got some counseling. At first they agreed, but then they became angry because they felt we were not doing enough for them. Their language became very "I" centered, and we realized that either this couple had never moved past the child stage or they had taken some steps backward. (It's possible to backslide. I wish we always kept the ground we took in the past, but oftentimes on our faith journey we stumble and fall.) We met with them and tried to help, but as I said they left the church.

When they met with me six months later, they told me what had been going on. They realized that the grass wasn't greener anywhere else and that they had become very self-centered. They asked for forgiveness for being so angry and told me that they realized that people were the same in the other churches they visited. They realized that no one had done anything on purpose to hurt them. They now knew that they had needed to step back from ministry to get things right again in their lives, and they were thankful we had forced them to do it.

As I listened to them, I recognized they were once again speaking the language of a spiritual young adult. They had taken their eyes off of themselves and placed them back on Jesus. Of course I would make them jump through hoops before I put them back into a ministry position (remember, anyone can sound mature), but God had been doing His work on them. My job was to recognize the Spirit's work and join Him in the process.

As this story illustrates, spiritual young adults still struggle with their sinful nature but are motivated by the desire to glorify God and to love others as themselves. They want the world to know what Jesus has done for them and what He can do for others.

RECOGNIZING SPIRITUAL YOUNG ADULTS

Spiritual young adults are action/service-oriented, zealous, God-centered, other-centered, and mission-minded, but they often don't think in terms of reproducing disciples. They are more likely to attempt to do everything themselves.

At the beginning of this stage of development, they are starting to think about and look for places of ministry. Unlike spiritual children, who might minister to others but do so because it makes them feel good, spiritual young adults minister because they know it is what God wants them to do. These maturing disciples also believe they were shaped for a purpose. They have learned that they are a part of the church and have abilities that can be used on the church's rescue mission to hurting and lost people. They also understand that God can use their pasts. They see that He can use every scar others have given them as well as every scar they have given themselves.

Their priorities have changed. Spiritual young adults tend to see their relationship with God as the most important thing in their lives, and they want to know Him. In the past, they had no time to serve others, but now they make time because the things of God matter more to them than other things that used to take their attention and time. These changed priorities are also evident in their homes and workplaces.

When dealing with others, they try to look past faults to what lies behind the actions. Spiritual young adults are not as concerned about an offense suffered because they care about the well-being of the offender. Their own value is not a question anymore. They are becoming secure in Christ.

Spiritual young adults know and accept that service requires sacrifice. They understand there will be a cost to following Jesus, but they love Him and trust that it will be worth it. They know that He deserves our hearts for what He has done for us. They recognize that by joining God's team they have joined the war and that in a war we can get wounded. However, they are sure God wins in the end, and they look forward to the victory celebration.

However, spiritual young adults can be naive about how the Enemy works. They can be uninformed about the cost of living in the spiritual adult world because they have always been protected (if and when the discipleship process works as it should). In other words, they have not had to be the point person, as they have benefited from the wisdom and protection of a more experienced leader. Yet they have the right hearts and goals, and it is precisely because of these characteristics that the Enemy has them firmly in his crosshairs. Like typical adolescents, they may need help but often think that they don't. People may even misjudge their maturity because spiritual young adults can look and sound more mature than they are. Consequently, they can get placed in ministry positions with little help for carrying out their responsibilities. Yet they still have some important things to learn.

In Matthew 17, we see just such a thing in the lives of the disciples. They had been doing ministry with Jesus for quite some time. They appeared to be competent, and in many ways they were. They had authority because they had exercised it when they had been sent out to minister earlier, but they were likely overconfident because they hadn't failed in any serious way yet. That was about to change. (Failure is a key component in the maturing process.) Jesus was ready to teach all of the disciples a humbling lesson to make sure they knew they were not yet ready to be on their own.

In this passage, Jesus takes Peter, James, and John with Him up on a hill and is transfigured before them. Jesus' inner circle blew it when they tried to put Moses and Elijah on the same plane as Jesus. A voice from heaven quickly reminded them that Jesus was absolutely different from Moses and Elijah. Then when Jesus came down the hill, He learned that the rest of His disciples had been unable to cast a demon out of a boy. They had seen Jesus deal with demon-possessed people many times, and they had even cast them out when Jesus sent them out to preach by twos (see Mark 6:13). But this situation was different, and they didn't realize it. Their faith and experience level was not yet at the place it needed to be if they were to succeed on their own in more complicated situations. Jesus talked with the disciples about what had happened and challenged them to grow in a couple of areas, saying first, "[This has happened] because you have so little faith. Truly I tell you, if you have faith as small as a mustard seed, you can say to this mountain, 'Move from here to there' and it will move. Nothing will be impossible for you'" (Matthew 17:20). Jesus went on to tell them that this situation was different and they would need to use a different tactic: prayer and fasting. Rather than get discouraged, they would need to push on through prayer.

I believe that Jesus knew exactly what He was doing. The disciples had become proud of themselves, and He allowed them to take on a new experience that would humble them. He was preparing them to be on their own (with the help of the Holy Spirit). Jesus knew they were not ready to handle **ministry** on their own, and after this experience, the disciples knew it too.

The beliefs, values, attitudes, and behaviors of a spiritual young adult include:

- Desire to serve for others' good and the glory of God
- Feeling responsible for how others respond to the gospel message; possible pride if a person accepts the message and possible discouragement if they don't
- Desire to serve but not strategic about how to train others
- Naivety about how well other believers are doing—for example, they believe that others are on fire for Jesus because everyone seems to be "fine" at church
- Being black-and-white about what should happen in a church

Some of the representative things spiritual young adults may say (the phrase from the stage) that reveal who they are include:

- "I love my group, but there are others who need a group like this."
- "I think I could lead a group with a little help. I have three friends I have been witnessing to, and this group would be too big for them."
- "Look how many are at church today—it's awesome! I had to walk two blocks from the closest parking spot."
- "Randy and Rachel missed group and I called to see if they are okay. Their kids have the flu, so maybe our group can make meals for them. I'll start."
- "In my devotions, I came across something I have a question about."
- "I noticed that we don't have an old folks' visitation team. Do you think I could be involved?"
- "I am ready to make disciples, and I will let you know if I need some help."
- "I am so exhausted. This week I called all sixty men from men's breakfast to see how they were."
- "I really blew it. One of the women in our group left the church. I must have done something wrong."

THE NEEDS OF SPIRITUAL YOUNG ADULTS

Spiritual young adults need:

- Help in finding an appropriate ministry to serve in within the church
- A spiritual parent who will debrief with them about ministry experiences
- Ongoing relationships with other believers that offer encouragement and accountability
- Help establishing healthy boundaries for their families
- Guidance regarding appropriate expectations of the people they will serve
- Assistance in identifying their gifts
- Help navigating complex ministry situations

Let's explore a few of these areas in more detail.

We have several young spiritual adults at Real Life who are serving as small-group leaders. We wanted to give these growing Christians opportunities to minister so they could mature, all the while understanding they may fail and make mistakes along the way. For that reason, we make sure they have plenty of accountability.

When we started Real Life, we had one small group. As the church grew, we had to try to keep up with what God was doing and needed more small-group leaders. However, the men who I felt were committed enough to lead were young in their faith and apprehensive about leading on their own. In order to give them the support and accountability they needed, I met with them once a week to go over the week's lesson and to discuss issues that had come up the week before in their small groups. We talked about questions that had come up that they didn't know how to answer. We discussed which absent group members they had called to check up on. We talked about how to train and nurture people who were in the spiritual infant or child stages of discipleship, and they told me who they thought was growing and could be apprentices to the small-group leaders.

After these small-group leaders had their group meetings on Wednesday nights, I called them to see how the meeting went. About once every six weeks, I visited each of their groups. This meant I needed an apprentice to lead my group while I was visiting their groups, so my apprentice also came on Wednesday mornings to our training time. It wasn't long until these young men were ready to become spiritual parents themselves. So you see we *can* move people into leadership if they have the right hearts and the right kind of support.

Keep in mind that children live in a comparatively black-and-white world, where decisions are straightforward and results are predictable. Eventually all of us find out that what was once simple is not so anymore. Like the disciples in Matthew 17, spiritual young adults will enter into complex ministry situations without knowing what to do or what advice to give. As these maturing believers start to minister, they often find themselves in over their heads, which is why it's important not to allow someone to dive into the deep end of the service pool without a lifeguard. Many times spiritual parents don't have time to keep an eye on those serving without a lot of experience. As a result, the ones just learning to minister can get discouraged or give bad, even harmful, advice to those being ministered to. When this happens, the Devil is right there to harass them, lie to them, and try to get them to give up.

Some of the most treacherous situations for spiritual young adults as they begin to minister can happen when they interact with fellow believers. Church domestic disputes are not much different from family ones. Police officers have told me that women who have been physically abused by their husbands will often attack the police officers who are trying to protect them from their violent husbands. Something similar happens in ministry. Many Christians have tried to step into situations to help, only to find the person they are helping starts to attack them. When this happens, it is natural to say, "Forget about it. I am not going to help ever again." At this point, even mature disciples need a spiritual parent to walk them through the situation and provide support and encouragement.

Young adults can also fall into formulaic thinking: *If I do this right, it will work; and if it doesn't work, I must have failed in some way.* Remember, they are naive. They believe that people will of course appreciate their efforts to help. I often tell developing shepherds that sheep, though cute, often stink. And they bite as well. A spiritual parent can help spiritual young adults avoid cynicism and discouragement by reminding them that in all of life, there is God's part, my part, and the other person's part and that we are responsible for doing only our part (see chapter 6).

Some spiritual young adults so like the idea of serving that they cannot maintain proper boundaries that will protect them and their homes. At the same time, other Christians so like the idea of being served that they use the inexperienced good-hearted leader inappropriately. If this is allowed to go unchecked, the results are strained marriages, wounded families, and hurting Christians. Spiritual young adults face burnout because of the things I have mentioned already but also because they don't know when to say no to leaders in the church who need volunteers but don't know how to protect them from overwork and use.

One other caution: Sometimes when spiritual young adults are put into the leadership of a ministry, the ministry grows and people are drawn to them because of their natural abilities and servant's hearts. However, keep in mind that spiritual young adults don't naturally produce disciples who can disciple others. They serve people but do not train them, so the load on the young adult gets bigger and bigger. As their ministry grows and these young adults minister to those under their care, they can quickly be swimming in water way over their heads. They may feel proud because their ministry grew, or they may feel discouraged because they can't keep up with it. Either response is a problem, which is why spiritual young adults need spiritual parents to help them process what is happening in their area of ministry and establish boundaries for the kinds of ministry they should or should not be involved with.

WHAT TO DO WITH SPIRITUAL YOUNG ADULTS

There are several things the disciple-maker will want to focus on when working with spiritual young adults. To start with, we must remember we are teaching these maturing disciples to increasingly fend for themselves. We don't want to hand out all the answers. Rather, we want to point people to where the answers can be found.

While it's okay for spiritual children to give simple answers to simple spiritual questions, young adults need to know more. They are entering into the deep end of the theological pool. They must be able to carry on conversations with non-Christians who are not only against Jesus but also believe misperceptions and outright falsehoods about Him. They need to be able to speak with mature disciples or with those who think they are mature because they can use big theological words. Young adults also need to know some of the key historical differences among Christians that have led to battles within the church, such as the theological differences between Baptists and Methodists, Catholics and Protestants, and so on.

Spiritual parents also need to remind those we are discipling that the endgame for every disciple is learning to disciple another. We need to help them understand that it is time for them to start watching *how* we are doing what we are doing — to teach them a reproducible process for discipling others, such as the SCMD process.

Because church is a team sport, it is important that the spiritual young adults understand the values and structure of their church. He or she should understand that the two of you (or your small group) are part of a larger team, working together to achieve the same goal. For example, at Real Life we have a community pastor who oversees several coaches, who in turn oversee and support all of the small-group leaders. Each small-group leader is training a future leader we call an apprentice. In addition, every leader in our church must go through a class on joining the team and a class on discipleship training. Our leadership training class is for all emerging leaders and is by invitation only. When our leaders at any level see another potential leader, they are to recommend that the potential leader be invited to take the leadership training class. Being a leader is not a status thing; it is a privilege and responsibility to serve those we oversee. Just as Jesus gave up His life for His sheep, we care for the sheep that He has allowed us to serve. They are *His* sheep, not ours.

So what is the disciple-maker to do? Once again, the definition of a disciple — and its focus on head, heart, and hands — can help us develop a game plan for what to do in order to train spiritual young adults in ministry and help them grow and mature.

A disciple is one who follows Jesus (head), is being changed by Jesus (heart), and is committed to the mission of Jesus (hands).

Help Them Understand Ministry (Head)

I want to make sure the young adults I lead are starting to understand some key issues about ministry. Again, the following lists are simply a place to start. We learn best by doing, and I believe that spiritual young adults learn best when they are being allowed to minister. (In fact, the SCMD discipleship process implies that we are all "learning doers.")

At Real Life we help spiritual young adults understand ministry by teaching them how to:

Defend the Gospel

- Teach them how to discern when to speak and when to be silent, and whether or not someone is really seeking the gospel.
- Teach them basic information about apologetics, the importance of not arguing anyone into the faith, and how to refute the basic attacks against Christianity.
- Give them an overview of the basic variations of evangelical Christianity (charismatic, noncharismatic, and so on).

- Teach them the key doctrines of the Christian faith and how to explain each doctrine accurately.
- Help them discern between salvation issues and nonsalvation issues.
- Give them an overview of common cults and what they teach.
- Explain how to answer complex questions, such as "Why do bad things happen?"

Work Under and with the Leadership of the Church

- Help them understand how their church works as a whole (the goals, the process, membership class, and so on).
- Teach them what it means to be accountable to their church leaders.
- Help them understand the big picture of ministry: reaching the area, the nation, the world.

Helping Them to Be Ministers (Heart)

Not only do spiritual young adults need to know the Word, key Christian doctrines, and how to answer questions and defend the faith, they need do so with a humble heart. The right answer given in the wrong way is still wrong.

Spiritual young adults must learn to *be* Christians, so we teach them how to defend the truth in love, confront with kindness and firmness, and be a peacemaker who fights for the right things and does not fight like the Devil for the things of God. So often Christians want to punish rather than win over, and young adults must learn the difference.

At Real Life we help spiritual young adults learn to be ministers by:

Equipping Them to Be Courageous

We teach:

- When to confront (when to look past the fault versus when to take the fault on)
- How to confront (always in private, without gossiping before

and after, in a loving way, in humility and love so that you are not causing the person's flesh to rise up, in a way that brings peace to the church and glory to God)
- When to leave a church or relationship (not until after you have gone to the person who offended you)
- The need to be accountable and approachable, not defensive

Helping Them Learn to Work with a Team

We encourage our spiritual young adults to:
- Become people who value others because others see what we can't and can fill in where we are unable
- Give glory to God for whatever is accomplished
- See the gifts of others
- See the needs of others (noticing the hurting)

Teaching Them How to Be Disciplined and Responsible

Spiritual parents must be responsible, so we help spiritual young adults learn to:
- Follow through on their commitments
- Be lifelong learners
- Be financially obedient
- Structure their lives so they have time to serve

Give Them Opportunities to Do Ministry (Hands)

The life of Christ within us eventually needs to translate to what we do. Ultimately the goal of every disciple is that everything we know is seen in everything we are. Again, spiritual young adults can do some tasks without help. However, do not assume too much. Be sure you know the spiritual young adult well. The following story illustrates why this is so important.

Not long ago I called one of the couples who had attended Real Life for several years and were a host home for one of our small groups. I had not seen them at church for several weeks and wanted to check on them. When I finally reached them, I learned that they had been attending some other churches in our community. They were upset with something that had happened that I knew nothing about (nor did anyone else on our staff). After we talked, they apologized for not coming in to talk about the issue directly with someone on the leadership team. We ended the conversation with the problem resolved.

I wasn't happy, however, because the community pastor who was overseeing that area had not called this couple. No one from the church had even missed this host family. Why did the home group leader not take action? Or the community pastor? What in the world had happened that so many people had let this slip through the system? (Do you remember early on in this book when I said that we have made our share of mistakes along the way? I wasn't just saying that to be humble! Every system looks good on paper—until you put people into it. Wherever there is a person, there is a problem waiting to happen.)

When I talked with the community pastor, he was surprised he had not heard about the situation either. He told me that the home group leader was "a spiritual young adult" and therefore probably missed it.

"No problem," I said. "Just make sure we track this thing down and learn from it."

So the community pastor called the small-group leader, who then called the host home. The next day I received a call from the family that this had all started with. They were upset because they had been told theirs could no longer be a host home. What was going on? Hadn't this all been figured out?

Now I had another problem to resolve. While it is true that Real Life does not allow people who do not attend our church to serve in leadership roles, this family had apologized for the misunderstanding and we had already resolved the issue. So once again, we tracked down what had gone wrong. The pastor had *assumed* that the small-group leader would handle the original situation correctly. He had *assumed* that the small-group leader would call the family and say, "Hey, I heard you guys were struggling. What can I do?" He assumed this spiritual young adult could handle a problem that *he* (the community pastor) could easily have handled. Now we had some major mopping up to do, including some major debriefing with the home group leader. Too much assuming had once again caused a young leader unnecessary problems.

Spiritual young adults need to know how to do ministry—how to lead their families, how to work with spiritual infants, how to effectively lead a small group. To ensure they learn these things, we need to watch them lead and help them learn how to ask good questions in both a small-group setting and in one-on-one conversations so that they can begin to evaluate where other people are at. Spiritual young adults must learn to be intentional in their caring for others. We want them to shepherd on purpose and with purpose, which means we need to help them develop the skills they need to lead.

So we work on the following topics. Some are new and others are more of a review.

UNDERSTANDING THE STAGES OF DEVELOPMENT AND THE DISCIPLESHIP PROCESS (SCMD)

Leading a Small Group
- Asking good, open-ended questions
- Making phone calls to the missing
- Calling and inviting new people
- Making hospital calls
- Organizing people to make meals for sick
- Leading a prayer time
- Dealing with problem people in the group
- Teaching through Bible storytelling (more on this in chapter 13)

Leading a Leader
Most of our spiritual young adults are leading and many have apprentices. They need to know how to intentionally develop another.
- How to debrief someone doing ministry

- The need for authenticity and accountability
- Basic counseling skills
- How to confront inconsistent behavior

Proper Boundaries
- Establishing and keeping boundaries — taking appropriate breaks from ministry; spending time with Christ, establishing a rule of no private meetings with the opposite sex
- Helping them remember we are in a marathon and not a sprint

WHERE ARE YOU IN THE PROCESS?

As you have worked through this chapter, it is my hope that you have looked at your own life and asked yourself where you are in the spiritual growth process. Are you intentionally raising up other leaders? I hope by now I have convinced you that it is the job of every believer to make and train disciples who in turn make other disciples.What the disciple-maker does with a spiritual child is so important, as it lays the groundwork for all that comes next.

Chapter 11

RELEASING SPIRITUAL PARENTS: *DISCIPLE*

About nine years ago, Don and his wife, Sharon, came to our church, shook my hand warmly, and told me they were new in the area. Don had a soft smile and an encouraging demeanor. After the service, he and Sharon stayed and without even a word helped us pick up the children's rooms and load the trucks with all the equipment we needed for the worship service (we were meeting in a cinema at that time). On Wednesday Don called and wanted to know if he could pray for me about anything in particular that week, and he wanted to know what time we started setting up for church on Sundays. Over the next several months, I got to know Don well. As a spiritual parent, he had made it his life mission to help others grow in relationship and understanding.

Like Don, spiritual parents walk with Jesus. He fills them as they go, and the overflow of their walk with God spills into the lives of those around them.

RECOGNIZING SPIRITUAL PARENTS

Spiritual parents are intentional, strategic, reproduction-minded, self-feeding, mission-minded, team-minded, and dependable. They are not just biblically knowledgeable; they are filled with the Spirit, so they have a loving attitude and encourage others. They know the game plan — they understand the mission, the rules of the game, the positions on the team, and so on. They have mastered the basics and then some.

Spiritual parents feed and bathe themselves. They are not dependent on a pastor or Bible teacher to spoon-feed them every week. Sadly, a lot of Christians want to go to a church led by a pastor who is a dynamic Bible teacher because that is the only time they will eat spiritually all week. Consequently, they are starving for spiritual nourishment. However, if they are feeding daily on the Word of God, the weekend teaching is supplementary.

Mature disciples also know how to bathe themselves. They understand that when it comes to sin, the Word of God acts as scrub brush in our hearts. As a kid, if I came into the house dirty, my mother took me outside and came at me with a hose, bucket, and brush. She scrubbed me so well it actually hurt, but she had to do what she was doing to get all the dirt off. Similarly, God's Word often leaves us feeling scrubbed. It hurts because we need to feel bad; we are wrong.

Mature disciples come to church to be inspired and taught, but they feed themselves every day; they scrub themselves all week. Not only that, they have relationships with those who are younger in their faith, and they relate with these younger believers all week long as well. As they do so, they are helping to feed them and they are modeling how they should also be feeding themselves.

As a mature believer (not a perfect or completely mature believer), I try to have my own Bible study daily. I listen to other pastors and read their books because I know I need it; it is my responsibility to go to the spiritual fridge and pull out what I know my soul needs and then eat it. I listen to Christian radio — Christian music and about three sermons a day as I drive around our community. I am in a small group, and I lead devotions and pray with my wife and kids. If I am missing something that I don't know I am missing, I have mature believers around me to point that out. That's why accountability is so important.

Remember, discipleship happens when we are in relationship with other believers where real teaching, authenticity, accountability, shepherding, and training are part of our lifestyle. It's the responsibility of all mature believers to learn to feed themselves, then to feed others, and then teach them to feed themselves, and then to teach them to feed others—you get the idea.

Spiritual parents will find someone to disciple. They will actively **share**, **connect**, train to **minister**, and eventually release to **disciple**. We do not have to encourage them to do so or teach them how to do it. They know these things are the Lord's will for their lives, and they are compelled by the Holy Spirit to do so. The spiritually mature understand and care about the mission of God. They have His heart. They can't help but make disciples. They can't help but enter into relationships with people because they have become relational people. I know that sounds strange, but mature disciples don't even try to be relational. It just happens because that is who they have become. They listen to people in order to find out where they are on their spiritual journeys, and they join them in the process. They are intentional and strategic about how they minister. Again, no one is perfect. We all have bad days. But the Spirit speaks loudly when we fail, and spiritual parents then adjust their course back to the Lord's will.

A spiritual parent looks at people not only as objects of God's love but also as tools in God's hands. We are all here for a purpose and are responsible, with other believers, for our own slice of history. Spiritual parents are much like real parents. They see the next president or the next pastor in their little one. But unlike biased parents, we are led by the Holy Spirit to see the potential in others. They understand that God wants to use everyone's gifts and experiences, so they constantly think about how people they know could be a part of His team if they were saved or would grow up a bit. Spiritual parents are intentional about helping an infant, child, or young adult grow up to make more disciples. They think in terms of training and releasing so that the army of God can grow.

Spiritual parents love the church—the family of God—and the work it does to further the cause of Christ. They understand that the church is God's plan to beat down the gates of hell and that there is no plan B. They believe that when the church works correctly, it does this mission well.

But don't think for a second that spiritual parents don't get disappointed with the church or with leaders—they do. And don't think they always have positive feelings about it. However, they know that God is glorified when a church is united as one team, working together. Spiritual parents simply cannot—and do not—say they love Jesus but hate the church. They understand that sometimes the church (Jesus' bride) is unlovely—that her dress is torn and her face muddy. But rather than mocking the church and pointing out how messed up she looks or just walking away to leave her that way, they work to help cover her and clean her. Why? Because they love Jesus. They know that to love Jesus best is to obey Him and to love His bride.

Spiritual parents understand the strategic purpose of the church. They know that the mission to reach the world works in two ways. Some tasks are individual—person to person, one on one, each person making disciples as they go. Other parts can be accomplished only with the body of Christ, the church as a whole. Weekend services are times when believers come together to use their gifts to reach different kinds of people. Some work with children, others teach in youth or adult classes, some lead worship, and still others greet newcomers. We pray together, take Communion, worship together, and provide a place for the unconnected to come and start the process of building relationships with other believers. When we make the weekend services a priority, we make a statement to our children and the world that we are together and Jesus is our first priority.

Spiritual parents also understand that we can work together in many ways outside of the walls of our church. Perhaps it is to meet the needs of the old folks' home down the street. Or maybe we come together to have a community day to provide food and clothes to those who have little. Maybe it is to bring our resources and time together to do any number of things, but a spiritual parent understands the power of *me* (individually serving) and the power of *we* (together using our gifts)

The beliefs, values, attitudes, and behaviors of spiritual parents include:

- Thinking in terms of what a team (rather than an individual) can do
- Having a coaching mindset
- Wanting to see the people they work with mature and become fellow workers who love them but aren't dependent upon them to complete the mission
- Thinking in terms of how to help a younger believer take the next step in his or her development

Some of the representative things they may say (the phrase from the stage) that reveal who they are include:

- "This guy at work asked me to explain the Bible to him. Pray for me."
- "We get to baptize someone from our small group tonight. When is the next 101 class? I want to get her plugged into ministry somewhere."
- "Our small group is going on a mission trip, and I have given each person a different responsibility. Where do you think we should go?"
- "I realized discipleship happens at home, too. Will you hold me accountable to spend time discipling my kids?"
- "I have a person in my small group who is passionate about children. Can you have the children's ministry people call me?"

Keep in mind that people talk about what they love, and when spiritual parents talk about what God is doing with them, it is not bragging or name-dropping. Their humility is evident.

THE NEEDS OF SPIRITUAL PARENTS

A Team to Play On

Churches get new disciple-makers (spiritual parents) in two ways. Either we develop them in our own church (or spiritual family), or they come to us from a different church or family. If they are from our church, we have recognized them as disciple-makers because they are making disciples. If they come from another church and we see by their actions that they are possibly a leader, we must move them onto the team.

As I've said, at Real Life we don't allow anyone to enter into leadership without going through some training and an assessment process. (Your church doesn't need to duplicate our process, but I encourage you to have something similar.) The person must become a member of a small group, demonstrate he is humble enough to follow, and be able to live out the answers he knows in his head. No matter how talented people are, we make sure they are aligned with us in our core beliefs and goals; otherwise they may end up causing division on the team at a later time. Spiritually mature people are willing to go through this pathway to service and leadership. They understand the need for the church to be unified and orderly and do not have a problem getting on the same page with the church leadership or with graciously moving to a church that better aligns with what they believe.

Let me give you an example. A few years ago, a small-group leader told me he and his family were going to leave the church after the small-group season was over. He said he loved Real Life but could not stay. Before he became a leader, he had gone through our membership class and learned what our church believes and then signed a covenant that he would uphold our doctrine. He later took our leadership class that reviewed our doctrine and outlined our leadership responsibilities. Again he signed the covenant. But over the years, he had evidently started listening to other leaders from other churches on the radio, and his views slowly changed. Specifically he changed his view about one of our non-salvation nonnegotiable beliefs and felt he could no longer keep his view from becoming an issue. It was not a salvation issue, but for him it had become a nonnegotiable. He was letting me know that he would keep leading his small group for one more month (to finish out the year) and then go to another church in our area that was aligned with his view. He had not shared his new view with his small group because he had committed not to in the covenant he signed—he would not be divisive on nonsalvation issues. He did not want to cause some of his people to question our integrity and beliefs as a church. He loved our church and what God was doing there, and he cared about the bride of Christ and about unity in the body. He was showing himself to be a spiritual parent who cared about the church as a whole and about the spiritual children he was leading. I was sad to lose him but proud of him at the same time.

An Invitation and Some Direction

Unfortunately, some Christians feel that discipleship is their personal mission but that it is not one shared by their church. They often work behind the scenes because although they don't want to cause a problem for the leadership, they want to fill in the gaps on the Lord's team. They have often developed their own way of making disciples by using materials by The Navigators or other products developed by a parachurch ministry. They love the church but have often not been recognized as an important part of the church they attend.

So what do we do if a spiritual parent decides to come to our church? What does that person need? An invitation. These spiritual parents need to see that discipleship is a priority and that we want them to disciple in and through our church. We need to affirm them and at the same time help them understand our language and methods for making disciples. Our job then is to invite them to become involved and get them plugged into a process for training, assessing, and releasing them. They often have things that can help us further the goal of making disciples as well.

Spiritual parents also need direction. It is the job of church leaders to direct them to the place God has designed for them. Maybe they have specific skills and passions that make them best suited to discipling teenage boys. Or maybe they are perfect for teaching the younger women how to be godly wives. Our job is to get spiritual parents connected to those currently involved in such ministries. If no ministry fits a spiritual parent's gifting, maybe it's time to start a new kind of ministry. As I've said, the job of a coach is to get players to play in the right positions. This helps the team win and stokes the fires of each team member's passions. As people begin to disciple in a new area of ministry, more disciples are produced who will likely have the same passions. The end result? The team expands as well as the ministry. In this way, discipleship helps the whole church grow into the full stature of Christ (see Ephesians 4:11-14).

To Be Released and Supported

Whether they are trained from within the church or come from the outside, all spiritual parents need to be recognized and released. This recognition doesn't have to be public, but the leaders in the church do need to communicate that they believe in these mature disciples and acknowledge that they are ready to serve and that they trust these spiritual parents with the responsibility of discipling others. This official recognition changes the way spiritual parents look at the ministry they have just taken on. It underscores that it is a responsibility. Recognition gives spiritual parents confidence that they are believed in and will be supported if and when circumstances demand. At Real Life we have started recognizing spiritual parents in front of the congregation and having our church pray for them. (Again, such recognition can be dangerous if those you are releasing don't have the right heart and are unproven. The Scriptures tell us not to put our hands on someone too quickly [see 1 Timothy 5:22] because they may fall into the same trap that snared the Devil's pride [see 1 Timothy 3:6].)

Spiritual parents who are released into ministry need support, which means encouragement and accountability. At Real Life all of our leaders, including me, are held accountable for fulfilling our church responsibilities and maintaining our spiritual lives, marriages, and so on. The Scriptures teach that we must continue to be faithful, and our spiritual brothers and sisters help us be just that. What people are not held accountable to do, they will not do.

I want to be very clear about this: No Christian ever "arrives" spiritually. Every believer, no matter how spiritually mature, will always have room to grow and learn. For example, Galatians 2 tells us that Paul confronted Peter about being a hypocrite. Peter refused to eat with Gentiles while Jews were around. But when the Jews were absent, Peter had no problem eating food with the non-Jewish believers. I love that the Word of God shows us people for what they are: flawed. Peter, a significant leader in the early church, was not perfect, and he was not above the need for loving confrontation. All of us, no matter our stage of spiritual maturity, continue to struggle with sin. Paul knew this well when he said, "For I do not do the good I want to do, but the evil I do not want to do—this I keep on doing" (Romans 7:19). Paul was admitting his need for grace, his need for humility, and his need for accountability.

No believer grows to the point that he or she doesn't need further coaching. Humility enables us to grow. We always need to go further in the process of sanctification, and people will always be a part of that process. We never graduate past our need for connection.

Ongoing Relationships with Co-Laborers

Sometimes people mistakenly think that to be a spiritual parent means they will get close to their disciples and then when those friends mature to the spiritual parent stage and are sent out, they will lose their friends. So instead of making disciples, they form friendship groups. (People often call these "accountability groups.") Others just decide they won't get too close to anyone, so they have shallow relationships with those they disciple. Both reactions are a mistake. Some of my best friends are people I have discipled. Yes, I have a group of new disciples I am working with and they too are my friends, yet I have kept in great relationship with some of those who are also now leading their own groups.

When disciples move to the spiritual-parent stage, they need friends to whom they can be accountable and who will encourage them. We cannot just have relationships that are taking from us. We need relationships that give as well. This does not mean we don't receive from those we disciple even while they are young in the process, because we do. But all of us need long-term friends who really know us and can look into our beady little eyes and call us on things that need our attention. This means that we must manage our lives in a way that enables us to make long-term co-laborer relationships.

WHAT TO DO WITH SPIRITUAL PARENTS

Not long ago, a young man who had been part of another staff member's discipleship group asked me if I would disciple him. I said that I thought he was being discipled by the other person.

He told me that he had been but that he had been released to start his own group. I asked him if he thought he would always need to be discipled. He told me yes. I explained that a mature disciple was able to feed himself and that if he was ready to be a spiritual parent, he was now a co-laborer with me. I was not his spiritual parent. I told him we could keep each other accountable and help each other. I told him I could advise him on some issues but that he was a grown-up now.

So what do we do when our disciples mature into a spiritual parents? We release and support them in the ways I've described in this chapter.

When I turned eighteen, I didn't go out to find a new parent to parent me. Why? Because my parents had done their job. I was ready for adulthood. Similarly, when a disciple matures into a spiritual parent, the discipling process is complete. Mature disciples know what they need and they seek it out. When Jesus sent out His twelve disciples, He did not say, "Now go find another disciple-maker to follow." He sent them together, usually in groups of two, working together in accountable relationships. They were mature, not perfect. It's the same for us.

Chapter 12

A FEW WARNINGS

Here are some pitfalls to watch for while discipling others.

WARNING #1: DON'T COMPARE BASED ON LEVELS OF MATURITY

Earlier I wrote that many don't understand the difference between usefulness and value. Let me write a bit more about that. Whenever we begin to address the stages of spiritual development and start to help people recognize where they are in the process, a few folks make the mistake of valuing people who are more spiritually mature over those who are less mature. Because of our sinful natures, we often become judges rather than supporters. This can play out in a couple of troubling ways.

One is that the spiritually immature think they are better than someone else because they have less visible sin. When this comes up in a discipleship relationship, I remind people that the closer we walk with Jesus, the more we are aware of our own failings and the more thankful we are for His forgiveness and love. This keeps us humble and grateful. Further, Jesus made it clear that we are to deal with the sin in our own lives first so that we can clearly see to help others with their issues (see Matthew 7:3-5). The second way this can play out is when Christians make the mistake of valuing more mature believers over the spiritually young. While it is true that more mature believers can be trusted to do more on the team, they are not more valuable. Jesus made it clear that a child is as, maybe even more, valuable than an adult (see Matthew 18:1-4).

So we must remember that we are all children of God if indeed we are Christians. Our value is not greater or lesser because of the stage of spiritual growth we are in, yet the depth of our maturity does determine our usefulness to the Lord.

WARNING #2: DON'T HAVE PREMATURE EXPECTATIONS

Our goal is to help people understand where a person is spiritually so that we don't put expectations on a person prematurely. We would not expect parents holding a newborn to feel angry at the newborn for being an infant. Likewise, we should not get angry at a new believer for being where he or she should be in the process. When someone acts like an infant or child, we should be asking ourselves, *Is this believer a spiritual infant or child?* If that is the case, we patiently endure and encourage growth — the person is where he or she should be and that is okay. Remember, people do not grow up in a day. However, we would become a bit frustrated when an adult throws a fit like a child. In that case we must remind the person as gently as we can that he or she needs to grow up. Oftentimes the Holy Spirit will remind the person even before we do.

WARNING #3: DON'T PUT A SPIRITUALLY IMMATURE PERSON INTO A POSITION OF LEADERSHIP

Remember that it is difficult to know sometimes where a person is spiritually because Christians often come in the form of a full-size adult, with many gifts they have mastered in the world they live in. At times people can seem wise and savvy, but we must be careful. Before we place people in an important leadership position, they must have a proven character over time no matter what they can do with their natural abilities.

I think I have made it clear that some churches often make the mistake of thinking that because a person is knowledgeable in the Scriptures, he or she must be spiritually mature. Our present-day

American Christian culture says that to be a Bible teacher, you need a Bible college degree. When this is the sole criteria for a ministry position, it's easy to hire a spiritual brat, someone with little spiritual depth or maturity. That's why it's important not to place anyone in leadership too quickly because as the leadership goes, so goes the church. While spiritual infants have a hard time acting like spiritual young adults because they don't know what an adult is supposed to look like, spiritual children can be more deceptive. They can speak the language and discuss biblical truth, yet they can miss the point of the gospel. According to Jesus, this condition is possible whenever we strain out a gnat but swallow a camel (see Matthew 23:24). He warned that we can study the Scriptures but miss the point. The Scriptures are all about Him; they are all about relationship. Paul told us we can know all things, but without love we will still be a resounding gong (see 1 Corinthians 13:1). Love by its nature requires some type of relationship. When people claim to be mature believers but are without a spiritual family (a church) and purposely abstain from relationships with mature believers, they are spiritual infants.

Here's a working example. The other day I got a card from a man who had been attending our worship services. He wanted to see me to discuss some "important theological issues." When I met with him, I did what I try to do when I meet with people: I asked questions and listened.

As soon as we met, he did a bit of name-dropping to make sure I knew he had a doctorate from a major seminary and an impressive list of friends. He spent the first several minutes giving me his credentials before he proceeded to critique our weekend service, from the music to the sermon. He said he noticed we talked a great deal about home groups, which he felt were dangerous because improper doctrine could be taught. While I agreed that without accountability this was possible, I felt there was a deeper issue in play.

I asked him if he had any relationships in his life that he trusted. He told me that there were just a few people he spent any time with. Mostly it was just him and his wife. In so many words, he told me he believed that Christianity was about God and himself; people were a problem for him—they were dangerous. Obviously he had been hurt. He didn't seem to agree with much of what we did, so I asked why he wanted to meet me. He said he would like to teach in our church. When I asked him why *our* church, he said that he had been to most of the other churches in the area and they were just too far away from the truth as he saw it. He also implied that not enough people attended those churches, so it wouldn't be worth his while to teach there.

I tried to be kind when I told him the first step to becoming involved at Real Life was taking our membership class. I shared that our team had to be aligned in purpose and philosophy as well as in essential doctrine. I then told him that the next step would be our discipleship class, which explained our definitions and methodologies for making disciples. Finally I told him that he would have to be in a small group and learn to shepherd people by caring for them. I told him the best way to teach was in relationship not lecture. He assured me he had been through enough classes in his life, and he said he was far too busy to be in a group. I made it clear that everyone involved in the ministry starts at the beginning—no exceptions—and is in a small group.

I shared with him that we believe that the teachers must be spiritually mature, not just knowledgeable about the Bible. Maturity is not just abstaining from sin or obtaining knowledge or facts about the Bible, but it is best exemplified by our love and service. Not everyone is naturally outgoing, but with the help of the Holy Spirit, we can all be transformed into relational people—more loving, gentler, kinder, and so on.

He disagreed, and our meeting ended. He eventually found a church that allowed him to teach a Bible class, but I doubt he is making disciples.

WARNING #4: DON'T FORGET THAT WE CAN ALL HAVE A BAD DAY

When we at Real Life help people understand the spiritual stages and assess where they are in them, one of two things typically happens.

They either overshoot their maturity level or underestimate it. We all can struggle with self-awareness. When they overestimate their status, pride sets them up for a fall. When they underestimate, the church misses out on a needed part of the team. A humble, honest person will often clearly see the times in his life when he has stumbled. The Devil loves to point out a person's weakness so that he will stay on the bench . . . what a shame.

At Real Life we have learned that *any* Christian can have a bad day and can say or do something that does not reflect spiritual maturity. This is a good reason why we must not make snap judgments about people we have just met or spent little time with. Perhaps they were a mature believer for years but are dealing with severe doubts as a result of a tragedy or some other issue. They may slip into the flesh for a moment but it is not who they are consistently. We don't always know what is going on in people's lives. That is why relationship is so important. When we have an ongoing connection with others, we can see how they deal with life in general and not just in isolated moments. Christians can act like a big baby for a few minutes (sometimes several minutes) yet still be spiritually mature. When we know the truth about where they are spiritually, we are able to act appropriately to help people. We may need to encourage them to "hang in there" because we know they are in turmoil, or we may need to challenge them to grow because they may have slipped back into the child stage. We may need to just let it go because the Holy Spirit is already working on them—we don't need to pile on.

Mature Christians have a relationship with the Lord and are immediately reminded by the Holy Spirit, the Word, or fellow believers about whom they are. If they stumble, they seek to make it right. However, there is a difference between a person who falls in a hole and immediately gets out and one who falls in a hole and makes the hole a comfortable home. The only way we can tell the difference is if we know the person well.

WARNING # 5: DON'T FORGET THAT WE ALL HAVE A WEAK AREA

As we walk with God, we mature in our faith and our understanding about God's work in our lives. We come to believe we can handle whatever comes our way, but then life exposes a need for additional growth. This can be discouraging if we forget that we will always have room to grow, this side of heaven. The Bible is filled with stories of people that God used in spite of their weaknesses. Mark it down: We will never arrive, spiritually speaking. We all have areas we have not dealt with yet, which is why we can be mature in many ways but immature in others. Even spiritual heroes such as David and Jonah struggled with faith and obedience.

I have learned some things about myself as a parent of teenagers that I did not know until I got to this stage of life. I found some weaknesses that I did not know were there. As I am pushed into new phases of life that I have not been in before, I am faced with new ways to doubt and have to learn to trust God in a new way as well. I write all of this for a couple of reasons. The Devil does a good job of getting us to compare and judge ourselves and others. The Devil likes to emphasize extremes. He loves to get us to believe we are more than we are. He also likes us to believe we are far less. When we sin, and we do, he loves to tell us we are too spiritually immature to try anything significant. He loves to shut us up because of a perceived unworthiness.

That's why we need to have an accurate understanding of who we are: sinners saved by grace, tools in the hands of the Master. God loves to use broken people because that is all He has to deal with and then He gets the glory. We can be used in mighty ways because of His strength and the gifts He gives us.

Chapter 13

A CURRICULUM FOR SMALL GROUPS

In every training conference we hold at Real Life, one question is sure to come up: What curriculum do you use in your small groups? For the last two years, we have been using a Bible-storying method, called Orality, in all of our home groups.

I became acquainted with this method of teaching the Bible four years ago when I met Avery Willis, the executive director of the International Orality Network. We quickly hit it off because Avery has a lifelong passion for discipleship. He created the *MasterLife* discipleship materials that have been translated into more than fifty different languages and used in more than a hundred countries. He started his ministry as a pastor and then spent fourteen years serving as a full-time missionary with the International Mission Board. His biography reads like a Who's Who of Christian leaders. As we got to know each other, I recognized and understood Avery's heart for discipling others, but I was unfamiliar with the curriculum he used in small groups: oral Bible storying. Oh, I knew the stories in the Bible, but I came to see that how they are used in the life of a small group makes a huge difference in how people learn.

Over the next couple of years, Avery and I had many discussions about Bible storying—what it is and why it is effective. Avery told me that the Bible-storying method came about because a group of Christians began to recognize that although the Bible has been translated into many languages, many people in the language groups don't know how to read. For a long time this problem was addressed by teaching these people to read, using Scripture. This obviously takes years and was met with limited success. It also requires these people groups to take on our culture, a literate culture. We live and learn in a literate world, but much of the rest of the world lives and learns in an oral world. Do people have to become literate to become followers of Jesus?

During one of our conversations, Avery made an observation that grabbed my attention. He said that our American culture is changing into a more oral learning culture and that in many ways the American church is being left behind. He recommended that Real Life try using the Bible-storying method of teaching the Bible because even if people like learning through reading, reading by itself is not the best way to move information from the head to the heart.

Much of what Avery said intrigued me. It sounded like something the people here at Real Life would respond to. To make a long story short, others on the staff agreed and we developed a trial program, using Bible storying in some select small groups with new believers and longtime church members combined. Before we knew it, we were receiving calls from people in other small groups in the church who had heard about some new thing we were trying, and they wanted to try it too. As we spoke to those in the trial groups, we observed that they were learning several things that were affecting them at a heart level. The Holy Spirit was using Bible storying to change their hearts in ways that we had not seen with other teaching methods or curriculum. Storying has proved to be such an effective way to teaching the Bible that we use it in all of our small groups now.

HERE'S HOW STORYING WORKS

I believe that unless someone is in crisis—broken and in need—we need to keep the Bible central to what we are doing in our small groups. At

Real Life we are careful not to allow our small groups to become counseling sessions. Although I want every group to be open so that people can talk honestly about issues in their lives, our leaders are not trained counselors. We tell them that if someone in the group brings up an issue that is too personal and complex, they should direct that person to a pastor or a trained Christian counselor. We try to train our small-group leaders to know the difference between a small group for the purpose of discipleship and a counseling group session or a whining session disguised as prayer time. There is a balance between staying the course no matter what (on the curriculum) and being Spirit-led as the situation demands.

Keep in mind that no curriculum works by itself in the process of discipleship. A person can't know the Word well if all he or she is doing is spending an hour a week discussing it. Disciples need to have a personal study time and be encouraged to bring questions about what they are learning to the small group or to a spiritual parent.

One more thing: At Real Life, targeting and training leaders is a very important part of the process, even more so than the curriculum. Here is why. We see the disciple-makers much like builders building a house. They have several tools in their tool belt that they have learned to use in the proper way at the proper time over years of experience. They know when to bring out a level or a hammer or a screwdriver. On the other hand, if the builder doesn't use the hammer correctly, there is a problem. It's true that without the hammer, the builder will struggle to be successful, but the hammer in the hands of a builder who doesn't know how to use it is a bigger problem. In the case of storytelling, we are talking about the Bible, so we can take this analogy only so far. It is the inspired Word of God, and it is powerful and effective, like a double-edged sword. However, if the leader doesn't use the Word correctly, he or she will pull things out of context or twist the words to mean something they really don't. We believe that the Bible is the best curriculum available, but we also believe that having trained leaders with the Bible in their hands is God's best way of making disciples. The Bible by itself is still missing something: a disciple-maker who trains up reliable people able to train up others.

That being said, here's how we use storying. Our pastoral team meets and chooses a story set for the year that we think is relevant for our people and what they are dealing with. This is called a biblical arc. Three years ago, we did a walk through the Bible from the Old Testament to the Cross. The next year, we went through the gospels, showing what Jesus did to train up disciples. This year we are going through the book of Acts. Every week the small-group leaders learn one of the stories to tell or they assign someone in their group to learn the story. The assigned storyteller learns the story so that he or she can tell it without reading it — not word for word but so the story remains true to the meaning. While the storyteller is telling the story, the small group reads along to see if the storyteller has missed anything. When the story is finished, the storyteller or the leader of the group will rebuild the story pointing out anything that was missed. The leader often asks someone to tell the story back to everyone without reading it. No one knows who will be asked, so everyone pays attention just in case he or she is chosen.

Once the story has been told, rebuilt, and told again, the small-group leader asks questions that draw out the important truths in the story. For example:

- "What new thing did you discover in the story that you did not know before?"
- "What did you learn about God?"
- "What did you learn about people?"
- "Which person is most like you in the story?"
- "What will you take away from this discussion?"
- "What will you do with what you have learned?"

We have the group leader or the apprentice lead the discussion time because facilitation takes some skill. The question-and-answer time leads to great discussion and application points for the group members. I believe that Bible storying is the best curriculum for the seven hundred small groups at Real Life.

EIGHT REASONS I LOVE BIBLE STORYING

Let me close this chapter with eight reasons why I love this method of teaching.

1. It helps our people know the Bible.

A story sticks in people's minds, while a verse (where it is and exactly what it says) can be forgotten. Bible storying helps people understand how they can use Bible stories when they are asked spiritual questions at work or home. Storying is a very effective, nonthreatening way to communicate biblical truth. Because you read stories in context and in order, people learn how the biblical story lays out historically. So many people do not know that Moses came after Abraham, or that David came after King Saul. It has really helped our people learn the Bible in a simple and effective way.

2. It helps us recruit leaders.

Many people resist leading a small group because they don't believe they are qualified to teach the Bible. In their minds, they have to know Greek and must be able to teach like their pastor because that is the only model of teaching they have ever seen. The only thing they were trained to do in the church was to sit and listen. In a few cases, they actually got to be an usher. I love to explain that all a person needs to do is tell a story and ask some questions. If someone asks a question the storyteller doesn't know how to answer, all he or she needs to say is, "I don't know, but I will know by next week." Because small-group leaders are responsible to spiritual coaches and those coaches to community pastors (in some cases volunteer pastors), small-group leaders get help finding the answers. Because storytelling is part of the human experience, most people believe they are able to tell a Bible story. And because they don't memorize the stories word for word, they are not intimidated.

3. It is better for real learning.
This method meets more people where they live. Because we rebuild the story with all the facts and because the listeners are participating, they remember the story. In the question-and-answer time, they apply the story practically to their lives and have something to work on during the week.

4. It better arms our people for service.
When believers learn a story, they are able to use it in a variety of ways. For example, the other day one of our people was at the hospital witnessing to his dying uncle. His uncle told him that after wasting his life, he had no right to ask God to save him now. At that point, my friend told him the story of the farmer who went out to find workers in the morning, midmorning, midday, and midafternoon (see Matthew 20:1-16). When it came time to pay the guys, he paid them all the same. Of course this bothered the guys who had worked all day, but Jesus reminded them that he had been totally fair to them, it was his money, and so on. This story gave the dying uncle hope, and he gave his life to the Lord. If believers are armed with a story they can tell from Scripture, they are better able to witness, serve, and disciple.

5. It helps our people disciple their kids.
Many parents believe it's their job to bring their kids to church and the youth staff's job to disciple them. These parents do not disciple their kids because they don't know how. But one hour a week in youth group cannot counteract all that our culture teaches our kids.

This is changing at Real Life because we encourage the parents in our small groups to tell the same stories to their kids during the midweek. And they do because it is easy. This has had a profound effect on our families. It has brought them together, and our kids are learning the Bible. Let me give you just one example of this.

Last year one of our small-group leaders assigned a member to tell the story the following week. The member took the responsibility seriously and started reading the story the next evening. A few days later, he started telling the story to his wife. His seventeen-year-old son, who had wandered from the faith a few years before, heard his father telling the story to his mom and wanted to know what was going on. The dad told the son about the assignment given to him and that he was nervous about telling the story to their small group and so he was practicing. The next night, his wife had to work, so he asked his son if he could practice on him. The son agreed. He told the story, and his son had the Bible open making sure he didn't miss anything. He and his wife had been praying for their son for some time and had been unable to talk with him about God without conflict, so this was a huge encouragement to them. Every day the rest of that week, the dad told his son the story and had the son correct him if he made any mistakes.

The evening the dad was supposed to tell the story to his small group, he asked the son if he wanted to come to listen. The son agreed. As the meeting began, the father got a business call he had to take and stepped outside. The call took longer than expected, and when he came back into the room, he walked in on his son telling the story in his place. His son didn't see him come back in, but the small-group leader did. He just winked at the dad and let the son finish.

Afterward the leader began to ask questions about the story, and to the father's surprise and delight, the son answered several questions. It was obvious he had thought a lot about the story. The next week, he asked his parents if he could come again to the group. It wasn't long before he received Christ during a small-group meeting. God had worked through a simple story and the faithfulness of a parent.

6. It helps our leaders assess where their people are spiritually.
Leaders who use the storying method to teach the Bible ask questions that draw people out, which allows the leader to hear the phrases from

the stages of spiritual development and accurately assess where people are spiritually. They are then able to deal with their questions and issues as appropriate in the group or call the people or meet with them during the week as needed.

7. It keeps our small groups from being boring.

Because our leaders do not use lecture and because storying allows for lots of interaction, time flies during our small groups. I can't tell you how many times I have looked up to see we need to stop because it's late. This sure beats constantly forcing yourself not to fall asleep.

8. People get to know each other.

Because people are relating to the story and talking, they get to know each other. They discover common interests, and they know when someone is hurting so they are able to better minister. They are also more honest about their sin issues, so they are able to develop trust and later accountable relationships that extend way past the small-group time. The result of this is life change.

Is it any wonder I am so enthusiastic about this method of teaching the Bible? Everyone can do it. No degree required. No performance necessary. We just teach our people to tell the story, to ask key questions, and then to listen.

For more tips and tools for discipleship and leading small groups, go to reallifediscipleship.com.

Part 3

LETTING DISCIPLES
EMERGE AS LEADERS

Chapter 14

FINDING LEADERS FOR YOUR CHURCH

Most people who study the church in America lament the fact that the church has a crisis in leadership. Many of today's churches are looking for leaders, but few are being found. Without effective leadership, the church flounders. Yet when I read the Scriptures, I see that God promises He will supply all we need to complete the mission He gave us (see Matthew 16:18; Romans 12:4-8; Philippians 4:19). I also see that many leaders emerged in the early church and were used by God to do great things. If this is true—and leadership is needed—what is the problem? I believe one problem is that we have redefined leadership in such a way that we are looking for the wrong thing. We are looking for men who can entertain or teach rather than men who can lead. I believe that the way we do church does not allow leaders to emerge—some serve and most sit and watch. This is why I call the church a show. To create a church culture that produces leaders at every level, including organizational leaders who can lead effective large movements, requires a clear understanding of the difference between spiritual parents and organizational leaders.

God gives specific gifting to people in the church in order to help the church work together effectively—to organize it into a disciple-making factory. One of those gifts is the ability to think organizationally. The Bible calls this gift the gift of leadership or administration. In other words, everyone is a disciple, everyone should grow to become a spiritual parent who can disciple others, but not everyone is a gifted organizational leader. I believe that if the church did its job correctly, leaders of every type would emerge.

Here's a case in point. One Sunday I lovingly and laughingly complained from the pulpit about a small-group leader who had baptized seventeen people without mentioning it to the church leadership for several weeks. I was excited that our people were sharing their faith, but I felt that the church as a whole needed to know what was going on. I asked our coaches and community pastors to do a better job of debriefing their small-group leaders about what was happening in their groups and then letting the leadership know so that we could share the good news with the whole body.

After the worship service, Pete came up to me with tears in his eyes. "Jim, I am so sorry for what I have done. Last year we had eleven baptisms in my small group and I never told anyone in leadership about it."

I hugged him and said, "Pete, I never meant to make you feel bad for that. I am so proud of you." He gave me the list of names and told me where he thought each one was at spiritually. Pete is one of the most gifted one-on-one and small-group disciple-makers I have ever met. He is about seventy years old and has been making disciples for years. In fact, many people he has influenced are now in full-time ministry.

Later I went to Pete's community pastor and told him to consider Pete as a small-group coach. Turned out to be a really bad idea.

The next year we moved Pete from small-group leader to coach and gave him three small-group leaders to oversee. His responsibility was to train the leaders to do what he had been intuitively doing in his own small group and to work with the community pastor so that his small groups would remain connected to the church as a whole. This role required some organizational leadership and administrative duties, which were new responsibilities for Pete. It wasn't long until he was discouraged, and the three leaders he was supposed to work with were frustrated as well. We saw these problems coming early on, and our community pastor tried to help Pete with his administrative responsibilities, but Pete just couldn't function as an administrator. He wasn't great at communicating to his leaders about the bigger picture of what was happening at Real Life or what was expected in our small groups by the church leadership as a whole. He was spending too much time going to the hospitals praying for people, sharing his faith with his neighbors, and counseling people in their marriages to be able to develop leaders in the small groups he oversaw.

How can I say that *anyone* spends too much time pastoring? Sounds like by any measure that Pete was a great leader.

Well, almost. Pete was a great *pastor* but not a great organizational leader. In the position of a home group leader, he was perfect. In the position of an organizational leader, he was hurting the team. His lack of organizational leadership skills meant that the apprentices in the groups were not being trained because the small-group leaders weren't being developed and taught how to train the apprentices. Pete was keeping his leaders from being leaders. He was doing everything himself, and he certainly wasn't taking care of the details for and with his leaders.

In short order we made him a small-group leader again. Before long he was leading the small-group members to spiritual maturity. From time to time, he would come to me and say he thought someone in his group had the gift of leadership, and more often than not he was right. We moved someone who had more of an administrative bent into the coaching position we had removed Pete from, and before long people in all the groups were growing again.

Pete was happy and so were we.

As Pete's story shows, not every spiritual parent makes a good organizational leader in the church. Not everyone has the gift of leadership.

THE GIFT OF LEADERSHIP

We thought that because leadership came easy to us, it would be easy for others. At Real Life we learned the hard way that our organizational leaders must be mature spiritual parents who have the God-given abilities and spiritual gifts of leadership. You might ask at this point, so what makes an organizational leader? Well, organizational leaders have an understanding of God's goals for the church and are able to create a structure that produces the values God intended the church to have. They lead the church to the right goal (making disciples), in the right way (a discipleship process), for the right reason (the glory of God).

God has given some people natural leadership abilities from the womb and has provided them with experiential leadership training in life. When they are born again, He takes these innate spiritual gifts and uses them for His glory in the church. The Bible teaches that we are saved for good works which God *planned* for us to do (see Ephesians 2:10). He saved us for eternity, yes, but He also saved us for His cause in this life. Romans 8 and 1 Corinthians 12, among other passages, tell us that God gives us spiritual gifts, and leadership (administration) is listed among them. God is a God of order—and the church glorifies God best when it is orderly.

Keep in mind that while a natural leader influences people, he or she may not be spiritually mature. Too often churches allow those with proven leadership abilities in the secular world to become leaders in the church without assessing where they are in the stages of spiritual growth. The bottom line in business is money—number of products sold, share value, volume of customers. And when gifted but spiritually unready believers are put in organizational leadership positions in the church, they bring this thinking with them. They think in terms of giving, attendance, salvation statistics, and buildings but not in terms of making disciples. God may want these people to be leaders some day, but they must go through the maturing process or they can end up destroying the church they love, sometimes unwittingly. (Churches don't split from the bottom up; they split from the top down.) Certainly, churches must and should think in terms of some of these bottom-line things. But a godly leader leads to the right place, in the right way, for the right reasons. When people aren't mature disciples, they cannot value making mature disciples because they don't understand what one looks like. This leadership problem is where we are right now in most churches in America.

RECOGNIZING ORGANIZATIONAL LEADERS

At Real Life we are looking for and seeking to develop people who are spiritually mature and also have the spiritual gift of leadership. These folks have the potential to become strong organizational leaders in our church, the region, the nation, and the world.

I want the process of finding and developing good leaders to be simple and reproducible so that our church can become purposeful and effective at making disciples and leaders. Every church has a culture; an effective reproducing culture is created when leaders believe in something strongly enough to live out those principles in such a way that a positive peer pressure is modeled. Those who are a part of the culture promote, support, and protect the culture that in the end will help achieve the mission. By developing leaders at Real Life, we are able to plant new churches, send out new missionaries, and help our church's secular leaders earn influence for the glory of God in their workplaces. The result is a movement based on values rather than on the personality of one leader. Again, most leaders (pastors) organize the church, if it is organized at all, around their abilities and personality. A church that values leadership will have many leaders who lead together toward an agreed-upon set of principles and Spirit-led goals. If one leader leaves, dies, or falls, there are many more around to hold the church together. The values, not the personality of the captain, guide the ship. Yes, personality plays a part in every church, but Paul made it clear that we don't follow Paul or Apollos; we follow Christ (see 1 Corinthians 1:12-13), and each person does his or her part in the church.

Before I go into what I look for in leaders and what I seek to develop on our leadership team, I want to again point out that *everyone* is flawed. We all have weaknesses. We see the goal, but we all miss the mark in one way or another. No one is perfect and we all need grace. Our credibility does not come from our perfection; it comes from the fact that we are aware of our common sinful nature and that we are changing by God's power. We must surround ourselves with people who will keep us accountable. We do this because we understand that our weaknesses and temptations can explode into the very things that would take us out of ministry and give Jesus less than He deserves: glory.

What follows is a list of qualities that I believe are found in strong organizational leaders. Keep in mind that we will seldom find anyone who meets every single one of these criteria. However, if we know what to look for, we can also know what to work on when God puts people with leadership potential in our ministries.

Someone with potential to be a strong organizational leader demonstrates:

Godly Commitment

They are committed to their Lord, their family, and their responsibilities. They may be an infant in Christ, but they already show signs that they are committed to whatever they are passionate about. They are hardworking. They are self-starters and do not wait to be told what to do. They are also responsible and finish what they start. When they give their word, they do what they say.

Initiative

They take the initiative to do what is needed to accomplish the mission. Many people in the position of leadership find themselves in situations that could keep them from accomplishing the God-given goals of the team. For instance, the youth group has hit its limit because the room holds only twenty people. Or the church is out of space in its two services. A leader with initiative will seek out those who have dealt with that kind of problem before. They will not just sit as a victim to the situation or wait to be told what to do by their superiors. They figure out a solution. They think outside of the box and they make things happen. The only real box that we must live in is the one the Word gives us. We can't change theology (salvation issues), but we can confront the status quo the church has lived with for too long.

Courage

They are willing to fight rather than give up when things get hard. Courageous leaders are willing to lovingly confront people who derail the work of the church. They confront those who disagree with the already-decided-on biblical direction. They do not allow immorality to go unchecked. If people do not come to their senses about clearly inappropriate and sinful behavior, courageous leaders will make the hard decision. For example, if someone who tithes large amounts of money wants the church to go in a different direction, rather than allow that person this kind of power because of fear of lost income, a courageous leader will confront the situation. A leader must confront, even if the person involved in the confrontation will leave the church, all the while trusting that God will supply for His glory.

A courageous leader must also have the courage to deal with broken relationships on the team rather than just hope the problem goes away. Jesus made it clear that He will not accept our sacrifice (even our service to Him in the church) if we have an unresolved relational problem with our brothers or sisters. They understand that we can't expect God to bless our work (God adds to our numbers; God causes things to grow) if we will not be who God calls us to be. Many church staffs come to Real Life for training thinking that all they need is a new methodology to reach people. While methodology does matter, unless we deal with relational problems in a godly way, we cannot hope to reach the world. Before we do anything, we must be Christians. Christians don't allow bitter roots to grow up. Christians forgive, bear with, and so on. Christians don't let the sun go down on their anger because this can allow the Devil a starting place to climb into the lives of the leadership and thus the church as a whole.

Passion

Strong leaders care deeply about the cause they have committed their lives to, whatever it is. They care enough to do more than just complain about whatever they perceive to be wrong with the world. Leaders are like stallions: You have to pull the reins back to slow them down. I have met a lot of folks who want to be leaders and are passionate about what *others* should commit their lives to. But when it comes to their own lives, they are not willing to get in and do the work. A passionate leader is an active person who dives in with a splash and even makes a mess at times. But at least he or she cares enough to try.

Sometimes passionate leaders appear stubborn, and their stubbornness can look like pride. But we must look closer to see what is going on inside the person. Passionate people may feel strongly that the church needs to go in a certain direction because of their past experience or because the Lord has put something on their hearts. They cannot easily be dissuaded. They are able to influence others because of their passion. We may need to disciple them further or redirect them to come alongside the established goal of the church. We also have to pray through what they are saying because the Lord may be trying to redirect the church through them. Or we may need to point them to another ministry where the goals of the leader and the goals of the ministry are the same. But we must not assume they are wrong. Leaders are hard to turn (but not impossible) — that is an attribute of a leader. God may have made them for the goal they care so much about.

Focus

Leaders are able to remain consistent in their direction for years. That is not to say that they don't change methods, plans, or systems in order to better accomplish the goal. They do. But most real, effective ministry happens over time. Too often people move from place to place before real roots and effectiveness can be established. For a sturdy tree to grow, deep roots and a large support system must be in place.

I know there is much talk about pioneers versus settlers and so on, and if God wants to move people He certainly can, but many leaders leave in order to avoid true change as soon as the church finds out who they really are. Others leave not because their work is complete but because they don't know what to do to move the church forward.

They drop the "God told me to go" card and leave. Still other leaders travel from large church to large church, searching for the plan that will make growth easy. No true growth is easy. However, it is easy to come home from a church growth conference every year with a new plan to convince the church to follow. (Well, going to the conferences is easy, but churches are often resistant to such leadership because the last church-growth curriculum or plan didn't even last a year.) Effective organizational leaders go to the Word to find their methodology and then fight to live it out. To do anything well is a fight.

Leaders must get everyone on the same page no matter what system they use. Each season they will have personalities to deal with and problems to solve. They must be focused and consistent or they will fail. So when I am looking for leaders or developing them, I am looking for people who do not give in to feelings of boredom or discouragement. They do not get excited about every new thing that comes along. Their goal is set — to lead God's church to make disciples of all nations — and they are willing to stay the course.

Humility

Humility is one of the most important qualities a leader can have, for good reason. First, God opposes the proud and shows favor to the humble (see James 4:6). Anything worth doing in this world can be accomplished only with God's help. It would be bad enough if God were to take His hands off of us and say, "Go ahead without Me." But it would be far worse if God was directly opposed to us. Without humility, we cannot win on God's team.

Humility means we first live for God's glory and not our own. It also means we work as a team, where every person is just as important as every other person. Humble people thrive in a team setting. A proud person will kill the team most every time. A humble person will be approachable and accept correction because he or she knows that anyone can be wrong. Leaders who feel they are always right are defensive and create an unhealthy separation between the players and the coaches as well as among the coaches themselves.

Humble people are lifelong learners because they know that they will never learn everything. They know they don't see everything, so they need multiple eyes to see the holes in their own perspective. They allow others to help strategize, implement, and assess the plan and its outcomes. Humble people know they will inevitably fail along the way, so they accept accountability and encouragement and give it as well. In other words, a humble person is a grace giver because he or she has had to be a grace receiver.

A Team Mindset

When I look for leaders, I look for people who value the team and fit well on one. For a team to be effective, each person on the team must play his or her position well and must relate well with others. Effective teams have great chemistry in the locker room. Talent alone does not guarantee a winning season. When I look for a leader, I look for one who will make the workplace more fun, real, and connected.

When I think back about my days in athletics, what I miss more than the joy of winning are my friendships with the other players on the team. I loved winning, but winning was so much better with the guys. The task, no matter how glorious, isn't enough for me, and I don't think it is for many others either. Doing the task with like-minded, committed coworkers is what makes the work really fulfilling.

I believe that this is how God wants His team to function. He gave us the Holy Spirit, who not only helps *us* change but also gives us the ability to love, bear with, and forgive those on His team. Church leadership teams are to be known not just for our effectiveness but also for our love for one another. Winning is a result of the team acting like a team. It is the result of working well together, on and off the field. If we leaders don't love each other, our people won't love those they serve with either. As the leadership goes, so goes the body.

So just what does that look like? Effective leaders are aware of their own strengths and bring people onto the team to fill in the holes. No one can strategize, vision cast, team build, systematize and administrate, be a peacemaker, assess, pastor, train, educate, and so on all by himself. Good organizational leaders understand the value of each component, though they may not be the best people to implement or maintain that component. Good organizational leaders make sure all the ingredients are in the recipe and acknowledge that they need help in creating the meal.

Too often churches are one-dimensional. If the senior pastor is a teacher, the church will focus on that one gift rather than become, with the help of other believers, a multidimensional church. These churches revolve around the teaching. They do not provide a place for people to grow up by serving in a discipleship environment. People who attend such churches tend to be too busy to be in a relational small group. They love the pastor's teaching and are part of the 20 percent of people who have an auditory learning style. Such churches can experience a growth spurt as the pastor's style attracts certain people with the same bent as him, but the growth is not sustainable, nor does it mean the people are becoming spiritually mature.

Great organizational leaders value the team's winning over self-aggrandizement and personal fulfillment. This means several things.

First, they give God the glory for what He is doing through them and the team. They draw attention to Jesus, not themselves. They also point to the others on the team as the reason for success. They don't allow people to give them all the credit.

Second, they play whatever position they need to so the team can win. Too many leaders play only the positions they feel most passionate about and comfortable with. While God has gifted us for a specific position on His team, and we must play that part over the long haul, He is capable of giving us the ability to serve Him in a way that doesn't feel good to us for a period of time. By using our weaknesses, He gets the glory.

Third, great organizational leaders are thrilled when one of the team gets to be a part of remarkable things and gets the encouragement that comes from it. In other words, when a teammate succeeds and people praise God for that person, great organizational leaders are excited. They do not feel threatened when people appreciate others. For them success is developing those around them to the point that they can step back and enjoy the successes of others.

Fourth, great organizational leaders share the development, implementation, and assessment of a plan and its progress with those on the team. Leaders often bring a staff around them to implement the plan the leader already created. They don't ask the staff to help create the plan itself. However, no plan, in my opinion, is as good as it could be when one person develops it. Remember, people will not live and die for the leader's vision; they will live and die for only their own. The one way for the vision to become theirs is if they share in its creation in some way. Besides, we need multiple eyes to evaluate any plan and see its merit and its weaknesses.

An Ability to Think Through Systems

Great organizational leaders can think through a process that will produce what is desired. They know how to measure success and how to assess their progress. They are able to step out of the fray because they have delegated effectively and see how the team is really doing at accomplishing the God-given goals. Remember, many leaders are so busy doing all the work that they don't have time to step back and see what is being missed. Organizational leaders think in terms of putting people in the right places with the right job descriptions. They think through the responsibilities of each position so it does the job the organization needs. They also think through what it would mean for those at the "player level" to perform what they are asked to do by the leadership. What do the players need for training, equipment, and relationship to win? Leaders know by experience what it means for players to do what the leader is asking them to do. How can leaders know this? Because they have lived that way themselves, and they understand how it affects their lives — families, finances, free time, and so on.

Too often pastors have never been laypeople, so they don't know what they are asking of their congregation—to have a job, a family, and so on and still do crazy amounts of work in the church. The job of a leader is to help people live effective Christian lives in the world they live in. This does not mean that pastors shouldn't ask for sacrifice—they should. But effective leaders understand what they are asking because they have lived—or are living—that way themselves. They have organized the church in a way that allows for success in all the components of life. They care about the long-term balance and health of their players. They don't want them to burn out or suffer harm because too much was asked of their families. Remember, God is a God of order, and organization was His idea.

WHAT WOULD YOUR LIST LOOK LIKE?

You might value a different set of leadership characteristics than I do. That's fine. You don't need to agree with me, but I urge you to make a list of what you value in leadership and to think about how you would train yourself and others to become intentional in developing a culture that produces these kinds of people. If what you do is specific and intentional, it can also be reproducible. That which is unintentional is not. Before you put together a list, ask yourself if you model these characteristics. As a leader, you cannot ask someone to do what you don't. Modeling is also the best way to train someone.

If we discern that someone is an organizational leader, we must help that person grow through the spiritual stages of development and then train him or her to become the kind of spiritual leader God wants the person to be. Over the years, I have met many Christians who had leadership potential but were excluded by previous churches because they lacked the discipline to do what they had promised. In other words, they had been asked to lead but had not done what they had promised, so they were relieved of duty, so to speak. They came to our church, and after our team worked with them for a while, these people became powerful leaders. When their former pastors asked me how we could let such irresponsible people lead anything at Real Life, I would respond that they were not irresponsible — they were great. Of course, they would say that the people weren't when they were with them. I would then ask if they ever confronted the person with the character flaw they mentioned before they just took him or her off the team. The answer was often no. Sadly for them, they missed out on a great leader who just needed coaching. They missed out because they didn't have the courage to confront.

In order to create a "leadership development factory" in a church, the value of leadership must permeate the organization. People must understand and live out the values so that others are affected by a form of positive peer pressure. A leadership culture is one that has a shared set of values and goals and an agreed-upon and shared lifestyle. We'll look more closely at this in the next chapter.

To learn more about the leadership culture at Real Life,
go to thestoryofreallife.com.

Chapter 15

CREATING A "LEADERSHIP DEVELOPMENT FACTORY"

In the last ten years, the staff at Real Life has grown to more than ninety people. Only five of these folks worked on a church staff before. Real Life has planted six churches in the last six years. Only two of the point people in these church plants had worked on a church staff previously, and never as the point person for an organizational ministry team.

We're often asked how we develop such leaders. My answer is always the same: The leadership of the church must view its job as that of making disciples who can make disciples. You must also understand that God gives different growing disciples different abilities for the purpose of completing the mission. God knows leadership is needed and He wants to supply the need. The church must know what leaders look like and be looking for them to emerge. Obviously, when you do this, those who are gifted by God to be organizational leaders will emerge. Core values set the direction. Core values are those things that we really believe. We all live out what we really believe. We can say we believe some really cool things, but when someone looks at our lives—where we spend our energy and resources, how we react when we are not thinking or when no one but God is looking—the truth about our core values becomes evident.

Before we can make a difference in our churches, we may need to do some real soul-searching. We may need to repent. Many churches and many Christians have the right gospel message, but they have replaced the methods revealed in the New Testament with new ones. This intersection is where New Age philosophy meets the church: "What's right for you is right for you" and "What's right for me is right for me" mentality. Over the years, I have heard many church-plant gurus say something like this: "God has placed a church in your heart. Your job is to discover it." If by that they mean that the church you lead might use country Christian music instead of hymns, then okay. If they mean your teaching style might be exegetical or to use Bible storytelling, then fine. If they mean that God has placed a methodology for reaching a specific kind of people like drug addicts in an inner city, then fine. But God's leaders are supposed to seek God's design for the church, and His design creates disciples no matter what style of music you sing or area you live in. The Great Designer knew what He was doing. He knows people: He made them, He knows what they need, and He designed the church to meet those needs. When we replace His methods with our own, the church experience becomes empty. It doesn't change us or fill us.

If a church believes that the job of the church is to make disciples and that everyone who is saved is designed for a purpose on God's team, its leaders must make it their goal to create environments where people grow to become biblical disciples who use their gifts well and in an organized way in the body. As a church builds a system that provides direction, accountability, and the ability to assess progress and make needed changes, new leaders will be developed and placed in right spots within the system. Some will become effective leaders of their homes, and others will become great men's or women's small-group leaders. Some will grow to become leaders who need more responsibility within the church, and others will become leaders who can lead their own church or mission organization or whatever else God might be calling them to lead.

A SYSTEM THAT WORKS

At Real Life we do our best to make disciples. When people become believers, they are baptized and surrounded by other believers who help them go through the spiritual-growth process. They get involved in a small group, which is led, in most cases, by a spiritual parent. In the small group, they see people care about one another. Their questions about Christianity and the Word are answered through dialogue and modeling. Every small group has a leader, an apprentice who is being trained by that leader, and a host family that work together to build a loving environment for the spiritual growth of their group members.

New disciples also go through our church membership classes, which establish in the hearts of new people the beliefs, goals, and methods of our church. Our small groups then give them the place to live out the information they have just heard about in the classes. As they discover their passions and gifts, disciples often get involved in ministry opportunities in the church. Some go on a mission trip or help in children's or youth ministry. Others become a part of the "connections" team, where they greet and connect those who come to the church for the first time. Most will get involved in our outreach events as we minister in tangible ways to our community.

Over time they grow through the spiritual stages of development and become the disciples they were meant to be. This is reflected in their families as they not only become stable Christians but also stable couples and stable parents who disciple their own children. Through all of these opportunities and ministries, some emerge as organizational leaders. We continue to relationally and organizationally invest in them and place them in positions that enable the church to become a movement.

Discipleship—when practiced the way I have outlined in this book—gives everyone a place to play. It gets people off the bench and onto the field. And when people are playing the game, it is easier to see who is emerging as a true leader. It lets the church get to know people and see what they can do. Because all of this is based on relationship, we know what their families are like, what kinds of marriages they have, and what their weaknesses are and we can build a team around them with people they already know and trust. Having a place to practice takes the guesswork out of understanding who is an effective leader and who isn't. Courageous leaders address issues as they come up so that if mistakes are made, they are dealt with. True coaching principles are applied. True discipleship lets us see who can do what, who needs more coaching, and who is simply way out of his element. We need relational discipleship to make disciples, but we also need it to make leaders.

Without leadership, a team fails. Without leadership, a country fails. But most critically of all, without leadership, the church fails. And the bottom line? Without true discipleship, it all fails anyway.

HIDDEN DIAMONDS

In the first chapter, I shared that at Real Life we have seven key leaders who work under an executive pastor, who in turn works under me. Only two of these men had ever worked in a church before. The rest we identified and developed as they went through our discipleship process. Let me tell you about a few of them.

Brandon Guindon, our executive pastor, became a believer while attending college in Oregon, about two years before Real Life began. He didn't know much about the Bible, so he began to study his new faith with some of the other Christian football players on his college team. When he graduated, he was then offered a job as a manager of a medical office near where he grew up, so he and his wife moved back to Post Falls, Idaho, to be near his extended family. At that time, Real Life was meeting in a rented movie theatre, and Brandon began to visit our church off and on. As the church grew, we asked him if he would help lead a small group. He and his wife, Amber, prayed about our request and agreed to help.

Before long, the leadership team recognized that God was working in Brandon and in his small group. The group began to grow. Brandon started spending more time with me and Aaron Couch, the other founding pastor. The church was growing rapidly and I needed someone to take over my role as the leader of our small groups. Aaron and I asked Brandon to leave his job and become our first full-time small-groups pastor. This would mean a huge pay cut for him. Brandon felt unqualified, but we reassured him that we would help him grow in his understanding of the Bible and the job. After much prayer and discussion, he agreed to join us.

Over the next several years, Brandon took our small-group system from twelve groups to over six hundred. That sounds incredibly thrilling, and it was. But it also meant that he had to develop and train more than six hundred new leaders. During that time, Brandon suggested, created with our help and the help of his emerging leaders, and implemented a coaching system for the small-group leaders that would not only train them to lead but also pastor them and hold them accountable. As the small-group numbers grew, Brandon had to hire coaches who felt led to become full-time pastors. He approached men whom he had seen make disciples and had proven they had organizational leadership ability. He asked them to do what I had asked of him: pray about leaving their jobs and joining the staff of the church.

Real Life hired seven full-time community pastors over time who oversaw the small-group volunteer coaches who in turn supported the small-group leaders. These community pastors, except for one man, had worked in the secular world. One had been a cabinetmaker, another a saw filer at a local mill, another worked for AT&T, one was a cement worker, another was an auto mechanic, one a school principal, and another an electrician. Most had become believers only in recent years through the ministry at Real Life.

As we grew, the time came when I would need an executive pastor, and Brandon was the guy. He had proven his commitment to our church and his ability to lead. This meant that we would have to replace Brandon in his role of small-groups team leader. Who could possibly replace a leader who could lead so many people in a ministry that was this important? When Brandon had started, there were only twelve small groups at Real Life and no community pastors or coaches under him. Now the job was much bigger and far more complex. We would have to hire a man who had proven he understood discipleship as well as the ministry process of our church. The decision was easy.

Jim Blazin, the former cabinetmaker who was serving as a community pastor, was the obvious choice. Jim became the executive team leader for the entire small-groups system and since taking over the role has seen the groups grow from six hundred to seven hundred. He has made multiple hires from within our small-groups system. He also worked hard to improve the entire small-groups system that he inherited from Brandon.

About two years ago, one of Jim's community pastors came to him with a vision for planting a church in a town about forty-five miles away from Post Falls. Gene Jacobs felt that God was calling him to this task. About four years before, Gene and his wife, Christy, walked into their first Real Life worship service. At the time, they were separated. They filled out a visitor's card, and when we met with them, they told us that they were giving their marriage one last shot. If we could not help them, they were done. Over the next couple of years, Gene and Christy moved from simply attending a small group to becoming apprentices to becoming small-group coaches in our ministry. Over time, we saw God's call in Gene's and Christy's lives, so we approached them about becoming community pastors. Of course, this meant he would have to leave his job at AT&T and take a large pay cut. But after all they had seen God do in their lives, it wasn't a hard decision for them.

This couple was very effective in their ministry at Real Life, so when Gene told us about feeling led to become the point man in a church plant, we agreed to pray with him about this. Eventually we sent him to start leading Bible studies once a week in the area. As his group began to grow, Gene and our leadership team worked out a timeline of how the new work would be released to his full leadership. One year ago, the church officially started. It has four hundred people in attendance today. Gene has already recognized his need for help. He hired his first community pastor two months ago, a man who started helping the church plant as its first volunteer small-groups coach. The same story in slightly different forms could be told for the other five churches Real Life has planted.

God has done something here at Real Life that goes far beyond the craziest dreams of those who were involved in starting this church. He alone gets the credit for what has happened. The best we can do in response is to share the game plan God has blessed here in Idaho. We think it is biblical. We know it works because every day at Real Life we watch disciples who know how to disciple others share their faith with their friends. We also see new leaders emerge as they become leaders in this church and in other new and existing works around the world. It is my sincere prayer that you will purpose to become a disciple-maker as together we seek to build uncommon churches filled with uncommon believers for the glory of the Lord we love.

To learn more about what God has done at Real Life,
go to thestoryofreallife.com.

SUMMARY AND PROFILE OF EACH STAGE OF SPIRITUAL GROWTH

GENERAL CHARACTERISTICS OF THE STAGE

SPIRITUAL STAGE	
Dead	• Unbelieving • Rebellious
Infant	• Ignorant • Confused • Dependent
Child	• Self-centered, self-absorbed • Idealistic • Prideful • Low view of self • Interdependent
Young Adult	• Action/service-oriented • Zealous • God-centered • Other-centered • Mission-minded but incomplete in his understanding • Independent
Parent	• Intentional • Strategic • Reproduction-minded • Self-feeding • Mission-minded • Team-minded (unity matters) • Dependable

TYPICAL BELIEFS, BEHAVIORS, AND ATTITUDES OF THE STAGE

SPIRITUAL STAGE	
Dead	• Disbelief of the supernatural, or belief in many forms of the supernatural (multiple deities, interactions with the dead, superstitions, astrology, and so on) • Disbelief in God (atheism) or belief in the possibility of God (agnosticism) or belief in a different God (member of a cult or the occult) • Belief in one God but many ways to get to Him • Anger toward Christians or the church or family • Confusion about God, Jesus, and the church • Ignorance regarding biblical truth (spiritually blind) • Belief that the answers they are seeking lie in worldly prestige, power, fame, and so on • Belief that they are as good as anyone else so they don't need a Savior • Belief that they have done too much wrong so fear they can't be saved
Infant	• Ignorance about what they need and what the Bible says about life and the purpose of a Christian • Ignorance about or frustration toward Christianity and the church • Belief that Christians make no mistakes; unrealistic expectations of themselves • Belief that they are defined as the culture would define them • Worldly perspective about life with some spiritual truth mixed in
Child	• Excitement over having deep relationships • Disillusionment because of their high expectations of others • Belief that feelings are most important, which leads to spiritual highs and lows • Lack of wisdom about how to use what they are learning—for example, too aggressive when sharing their faith, or too legalistic in their approach to dealing with their friends and family • Belief that people are not caring for them enough • Tendency to mimic mature Christians' behaviors in order to look good and gain praise • Tendency to serve others in a ministry as long as the benefit outweighs the cost • Enthusiasm about new teachings • Confusion and unyielding nature regarding complex issues because they have an incomplete view of biblical subjects • More knowledge about what Christians say than what the Word says
Young Adult	• Desire to serve others for others' good and the glory of God • Tendency to feel responsible for how others respond to the message; possible pride if a person accepts the message and possible discouragement if he or she doesn't • Desire to serve but not strategic about how to train others • Naivety about other believers—for example, they believe that others are on fire for Jesus because everyone seems to be "fine" at church • Tendency to be black-and-white about what should happen in a church
Parent	• Ability to think in terms of what a team (rather than an individual) can do • A coaching mindset • Desire to see the people they work with mature and become fellow workers who love them but aren't dependent on them to complete the mission

THE SPIRITUAL NEEDS OF THE STAGE

SPIRITUAL STAGE	
Dead	• A secure relationship with a more mature believer • A picture of the real Jesus lived out in front of them • Answers, evidences for Christianity • An explanation of the gospel message • An invitation to receive Christ
Infant	• Individual attention from a spiritual parent • Protection • A explanation of the truths (new truths) found in the Word of God • An explanation and modeling of the habits of a growing believer
Child	• A spiritual family • Help for how to start feeding themselves • Teaching about who they are in Christ • Teaching about how to have relationship with Christ • Teaching about how to have relationship with other believers • Teaching about appropriate expectations concerning other believers
Young Adult	• A place to learn to serve • A spiritual parent who will debrief them about ministry experiences • Ongoing relationships that offer encouragement and accountability • Help for establishing boundaries • Guidance regarding appropriate expectations of people they will serve • Help in identifying their gifts • Skills training
Parent	• An ongoing relationship with co-laborers • A church family • Encouragement

THE PHRASE FROM THE STAGE

SPIRITUAL STAGE	
Dead	• "I don't believe there is a God." • "The Bible is just a bunch of myths." • "Evolution explains away a need for God." • "I am not a Christian because Christians are responsible for all the wars in history." • "There are many ways to get to God." • "I am a Christian because I go to church and I am a good person." • "I have been a good person, so I will be okay."

Infant	• "I believe in Jesus, but my church is when I'm in the woods or on the lake." • "I don't have to go to church to be a Christian." • "I gave my life to Jesus and I go to church, but I don't need to be close to other people." • "People have hurt me, so it's just me and God." • "I don't have time to be in relationship with another Christian." • "My spouse is my accountability partner. I don't need anyone else." • "I pray and read my Bible. That is good enough for me." • "My ministry is my work. I provide for my family. I don't have time for the church." • "I didn't know the Bible said that."
Child	• "I love my small group; don't add any more people to it." • "Who are all these people coming to my church? Tell them to go somewhere else!" • "I am not coming to church anymore. It has become too big; it has too many people." • "My small group is not taking care of my needs." • "I don't have anyone who is spending enough time with me; no one is discipling me." • "I didn't like the music today. If only they did it like . . ." • "I am not being fed in my church, so I am going to a church that meets my needs better."
Young Adult	• "I love my group, but there are others who need a group like this." • "I think I could lead a group with a little help. I have three friends I have been witnessing to, and this group would be too big for them." • "Look how many are at church today—it's awesome! I had to walk two blocks from the closest parking spot." • "Randy and Rachel missed group and I called to see if they are okay. Their kids have the flu, so maybe our group can make meals for them. I'll start." • "In my devotions, I came across something I have a question about." • "I noticed that we don't have an old folks' visitation team. Do you think I could be involved?"
Parent	*People talk about what they love. When spiritual parents talk about what God is doing with them, it is not bragging or name-dropping. Humility is evident.* • "This guy at work asked me to explain the Bible to him. Pray for me." • "We get to baptize someone from our small group tonight. When is the next 101 class? I want to get her plugged into ministry somewhere." • "Our small group is going on a mission trip, and I have given each person a different responsibility. Where do you think we should go?" • "I realized discipleship happens at home, too. Will you hold me accountable to spend time discipling my kids?" • "I have a person in my small group who is passionate about children. Can you have the children's ministry people call me?"

RECOMMENDED RESOURCES FOR DISCIPLE-MAKERS

By now you understand that discipleship begins and is sustained by relationship, not information. But don't be fooled. Disciple-makers must be ready to give an answer, defend the faith, and teach their disciples the truth of the Bible in a world determined to provide a different game plan than the one Jesus left for us.

The Bible itself should always be our starting point. And it needs to remain our "true north" for every step along the way. We are blessed to live in an era when many great resources for spiritual growth are available. Spiritual parents know how to use these resources, and they know how to help their disciples use them.

What follows is a suggested beginning place for many of the topics covered in this book. You will find other resources that are just as helpful. You won't know everything when you begin to work with people, and as you disciple people, you will likely find additional topics that need to be covered. You will find that even when working with a disciple at one stage of spiritual growth, you will often need to refer to topics already covered (or maybe not yet discussed). This list is just a reference for you, not a curriculum to be mastered. Add to it as problems and successes come. Make it your own.

You can find additional resources for discipleship at reallifediscipleship .com. Learn more about the history, rapid growth, and disciple-making culture of Real Life Ministries at thestoryofreallife.com.

SHARING WITH THE SPIRITUALLY DEAD

Unbelievers often have serious questions about complex issues. While our best answer is often our stories of how Jesus has changed our lives, disciple-makers must also learn to answer some of the tough questions spiritually dead people ask about our faith and life itself.

Defending the Gospel (Apologetics)

Geisler, Norman L., and Frank Turek. *I Don't Have Enough Faith to Be an Atheist.*

Habermas, Gary R., and Michael R. Licona. *The Case for the Resurrection of Jesus.*

Keller, Timothy. *The Reason for God: Belief in an Age of Skepticism.*

Little, Paul E., and James F. Nyquist. *Know Why You Believe.*

McDowell, Josh. *Evidence That Demands a Verdict.*

Strobel, Lee. *The Case for Christ: A Journalist's Personal Investigation of the Evidence for Jesus.*

Wright, N. T. *Simply Christian: Why Christianity Makes Sense.*

Authority of Scripture

Wright, N. T. *The Last Word: Scripture and the Authority of God.*

How Christianity Differs from Other Faiths

Ridenour, Fritz. *So What's the Difference?*

Stott, John R. W. *Basic Christianity.*

Dealing with Past Hurts

Arterburn, Stephen. *Healing Is a Choice.*

Bridges, Jerry. *Trusting God: Even When Life Hurts.*

Crabb, Larry. *Shattered Dreams: God's Unexpected Pathway to Joy.*

Yancey, Philip. *Where Is God When It Hurts?*

SHARING WITH SPIRITUAL INFANTS

Infants need for a disciple-maker to share life with them — to nurture and protect their new spiritual life. Part of that process will usually involve helping them see two key aspects of their new faith: the spiritual realities behind the world they see (or a biblical worldview) and how spiritual transformation happens.

Developing a Biblical Worldview

Colson, Charles, and Nancy Pearcey. *How Now Shall We Live?*
Noebel, David. *Understanding the Times: The Collision of Today's Competing Worldviews.*
Sire, James W. *The Universe Next Door: A Basic Worldview Catalog.*

Spiritual Transformation

Warren, Rick. *The Purpose-Driven Life.*
Whitney, Donald S. *Spiritual Disciplines for the Christian Life.*
Willard, Dallas. *Renovation of the Heart: Putting On the Character of Christ.*

CONNECTING WITH SPIRITUAL CHILDREN

Children are typically eager learners, and disciple-makers are wise to help them connect to teaching that will help them grow. Remember, we do spiritual children no service by spoon-feeding all these topics. Be a guide and offer suggestions. When necessary, help them digest the big pieces of what they are learning.

Who They Are in Christ

Bridges, Jerry. *The Discipline of Grace: God's Role and Our Role in the Pursuit of Holiness.*
Manning, Brennan. *The Ragamuffin Gospel.*

How to Have a Relationship with God

Blackaby, Henry, Richard Blackaby, and Claude King. *Experiencing God: Knowing and Doing the Will of God.*

Bounds, E. M. *Power through Prayer.*

Tozer, A. W. *The Pursuit of God.*

Maintaining Healthy Relationships

Chapman, Gary. *The Five Love Languages: The Secret to Love That Lasts.*

Eggerichs, Emerson. *Love and Respect: The Love She Most Desires; The Respect He Desperately Needs.*

Smalley, Gary. *The DNA of Relationships.*

How to Spiritually Feed Themselves

Fee, Gordon D., and Douglas Stuart. *How to Read the Bible for All Its Worth.*

Warren, Rick. *Bible Study Methods.*

The Importance of Connection: A Growing Understanding of the Church

Crabb, Larry. *The Safest Place on Earth: Where People Connect and Are Forever Changed.*

Scazzero, Peter. *The Emotionally Healthy Church.*

Willis, Avery, and Henry Blackaby. *On Mission with God.*

MINISTERING WITH SPIRITUAL YOUNG ADULTS

At this stage of spiritual growth, disciples have an expanding circle of influence in their ministry. As you disciple spiritual young adults, you might find that many of the suggested resources already mentioned continue to be helpful now, just at a deeper, more involved level of discussion and study.

Doctrine and Theology

Alcorn, Randy. *Heaven*.

Grudem, Wayne. *Bible Doctrine*.

Lewis, C. S. *Mere Christianity*.

McDowell, Josh. *More Than a Carpenter*.

Packer, J. I. *Knowing God*.

Piper, John. *Desiring God: Meditations of a Christian Hedonist*.

Piper, John. *Let the Nations Be Glad! The Supremacy of God in Missions*.

Church History

Jenkins, Philip. *The Next Christendom: The Coming of Global Christianity*.

Kennedy, D. James, and Jerry Newcombe. *What If Jesus Had Never Been Born?*

Stark, Rodney. *The Rise of Christianity*.

Life Management

Cloud, Henry, and John Townsend. *Boundaries: When to Say Yes, When to Say No to Take Control of Your Life*.

Dayton, Howard. *Your Money Counts*.

Sider, Ronald J. *Rich Christians in an Age of Hunger*.

Swenson, Richard. *Margin: Restoring Emotional, Physical, Financial, and Time Reserves to Overloaded Lives*.

Doing Ministry:
Leading Small Groups, Identifying Spiritual Gifts

Blanchard, Ken, and Phil Hodges. *Lead like Jesus*.

Coleman, Robert Emerson. *The Master Plan of Evangelism*.

Crabb, Larry. *Soul Talk: The Language God Longs for Us to Speak*.

Willis, Avery. *MasterLife: A Biblical Process for Growing Disciples*.

Orality and Bible Storytelling

Willis, Avery. *Making Disciples of Oral Learners.*
Willis, Avery, and Mark Snowden. *Truth That Sticks.*

SPIRITUAL FACTS

- God created us to be in relationship with Himself (see Genesis 1:1,26; 3:8-9).
- God gave us a choice: Did we want to be in relationship with Him (see Genesis 2:16-17)?
- God warned us about the consequences of rejecting Him, not believing Him (see Genesis 2:17).
- We chose to be our own gods, to choose our own right and wrong (see Genesis 3:8-9).
- Like Adam and Eve, we have all sinned and we all die (see Romans 3:23; 5:12; 6:23).
- There are two kinds of death (see Revelation 20:14-15).
- But God loved us so much that He sent His Son to save us (see John 3:16).
- Jesus took our sin and gave us His righteousness *if* we will believe (see Romans 1:16-17; Ephesians 2:8-10).
- What is faith? (see Romans 4:3 — to believe Him; Romans 1:5 — to obey Him).
- A person who believes repents and is baptized (see Acts 2:38).
- A person who is saved is being changed (see Luke 6:44-45; Galatians 5:22; James 2:14).
- The Word of God (the Bible) is our guide (see 2 Timothy 3:16).
- In the church (God's people) we learn what it means to be a follower of Christ (see Acts 2:41-44).

PRESENTATION OF THE GOSPEL

TWO CHOICES

DEATH

Revelation 20:14
Death and Hades were thrown into the lake of fire. The lake of fire is the second death. Anyone whose name was not found written in the book of life was thrown into the lake of fire.

MAN

GOD

- Rebellious
- Sinful
- Separated
- Dying

DEATH
- Physical
- Spiritual

- Holy
- Righteous
- Love
- Life

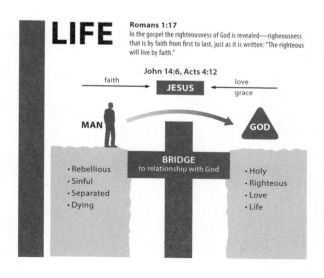

LIFE

Romans 1:17
In the gospel the righteousness of God is revealed—righeousness that is by faith from first to last, just as it is written: "The righteous will live by faith."

John 14:6, Acts 4:12

faith → **JESUS** ← love / grace

MAN

GOD

BRIDGE
to relationship with God

- Rebellious
- Sinful
- Separated
- Dying

- Holy
- Righteous
- Love
- Life

ABOUT THE AUTHOR

JIM PUTMAN is the cofounder and senior pastor of Real Life Ministries in Post Falls, Idaho. Prior to his role as senior pastor, he served as a youth minister in two small churches. In college, Jim won three All-American titles in wrestling and went on to become a successful wrestling coach. Real Life was launched in 1998 with a commitment to discipleship and the model of discipleship Jesus practiced, which is called relational discipleship. *Outreach* magazine has continually listed Real Life Ministries among the top one hundred most influential churches in America. Jim is also a cofounder and leader of the Relational Discipleship Network. Jim holds degrees from Boise State University and Boise Bible College. His voice reaches hundreds of thousands across the world through conference presentations, the web, podcasts, and weekend services.

He is the author of five books: *Church Is a Team Sport* (2008), *Real-Life Discipleship* (2010), *The Power of Together* (2016), *The Disciple's Journey* (2022), and *RelationShift* (2023). He coauthored four books with others: *Real-Life Discipleship Training Manual* (with Avery T. Willis Jr., Brandon Guindon, and Bill Krause; 2010), *DiscipleShift* (with Bobby Harrington and Robert E. Coleman; 2013), *Hope For the Prodigal* (with Bill Putman; 2017) and *The Revolutionary Disciple* (with Chad Harrington; 2021). Jim's passion is discipleship through small groups. With his background in sports and coaching, he believes in the value of strong coaching as a means to disciple others. He and his wife, along with their sons, daughter-in-laws, and grandchildren, live in scenic North Idaho.

You can learn more by visiting his website, jimputman.com, and by watching the story of Real Life Ministries at thestoryofreallife.com.

A FULL LINE OF DISCIPLE-MAKING RESOURCES

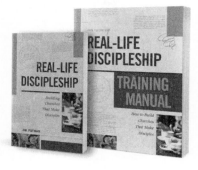

Real-Life Discipleship
Make disciple-making come alive in your church!

Real-Life Discipleship Training Manual
A practical, 14-week workbook for small-group leaders.

The Power of Together
Learn to live in authentic, relational communities—the kind that Jesus modeled.

The Power of Together Workbook
A 9-week workbook to practice authentic, relational discipleship.

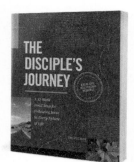

The Disciple's Journey
A transformative workbook for every member of your church.

CP2016

NavPress is the book-publishing arm of The Navigators.

Since 1933, The Navigators has helped people around the world bring hope and purpose to others in college campuses, local churches, workplaces, neighborhoods, and hard-to-reach places all over the world, face-to-face and person-by-person in an approach we call Life-to-Life® discipleship. We have committed together to know Christ, make Him known, and help others do the same.®

Would you like to join this adventure of discipleship and disciplemaking?

- Take a Digital Discipleship Journey at **navigators.org/disciplemaking**.
- Get more discipleship and disciplemaking content at **thedisciplemaker.org**.
- Find your next book, Bible, or discipleship resource at **navpress.com**.

 @NavPressPublishing

 @NavPress

 @navpressbooks